Using csh and tcsh

Using csh and tcsh

Paul DuBois

O'Reilly & Associates, Inc.
103 Morris Street, Suite A
Sebastopol, CA 95472

Using csh and tcsh
by Paul DuBois

Editor: Adrian Nye

Production Editor: Kiersten Nauman

Printing History:

August 1995:   First Edition.

This book is printed on acid-free paper with 85% recycled content, 15% post-consumer waste. O'Reilly & Associates is committed to using paper with the highest recycled content available consistent with high quality.

ISBN: 1-56592-132-1   [10/96]

Table of Contents

Tables

Preface

A shell is a command interpreter. You type commands into a shell, and the shell passes them to the computer for execution. UNIX systems usually provide several shell choices. This handbook focuses on two of the shells: C shell (*csh*) and an enhanced C shell (*tcsh*).

C shell (*csh*), a popular command interpreter that has its origins in Berkeley UNIX, is particularly suited for interactive use. It offers many features, including an ability to recall and modify previous commands, a facility for creating command short-cuts, shorthand notation for pathnames to home directories, and job control.

tcsh, an enhanced version of *csh*, is almost entirely upward compatible with *csh*, so whatever you know about the C shell you can apply immediately to *tcsh*. But *tcsh* goes beyond *csh*, adding capabilities like a general purpose command line editor, spelling correction, and programmable command, file, and user name completion.

Shells other than *csh* and *tcsh* may be available on your system. The two most significant examples are the Bourne shell (*sh*) and the Korn shell (*ksh*). The Bourne shell is the oldest of the currently popular shells and is the most widely available. The Korn shell was developed at AT&T and is most prevalent on System V-based UNIX systems. Both shells are fully documented elsewhere, so we won't deal with them here.

This handbook is designed to help you use *csh* or *tcsh* more effectively. By demonstrating what these shells can do for you, and illustrating techniques for using their features, the handbook will show you how to get your work done more quickly and easily. You can increase your effectiveness on a number of fronts, ranging from learning how to repeat the previous command without typing the whole thing again, to learning how to use filename patterns, to using the shell startup files to make your working environment more pleasant and productive.

This handbook has two particular emphases:

- *Interactive use of the shell.* Although you can use a shell non-interactively by telling it to execute commands contained in a file, you will spend more time with your shell at the command line. This handbook reflects that pattern of use by concentrating on how to improve your interaction with the shell rather than on writing shell scripts. Another reason for emphasizing interactive use over scripting is that *csh* and *tcsh* are not good shells for writing scripts (Appendix C, *Other Sources of Information*, references a document that describes why). *sh* or *perl* are better for writing scripts, so there is little reason to discuss doing so with *csh* or *tcsh*.

- *Special features of tcsh.* Most shell books mention *tcsh* only in passing, as an obscure relative of *csh*, or not at all. While this handbook discusses the many capabilities that *csh* and *tcsh* have in common, it also describes *tcsh*-specific features instead of ignoring them. In fact, I recommend that you use *tcsh* as your shell—it's just a lot better than *csh*.

Intended Audience

This handbook can be used by anyone at any level of proficiency with *csh* or *tcsh*. It should be helpful in the following circumstances:

- *You don't know much about the shell.* A simple introduction is provided that can help you avoid the frustration that can be a part of the early learning stages. If you're new not only to the shell, but also to UNIX, that's fine, too. Although this handbook isn't designed as a general UNIX tutorial, it contains many examples that show how to use UNIX commands.

- *You're already familiar with the fundamentals of the shell.* This handbook will help you get more out of *csh* and *tcsh* by demonstrating how to use their interactive capabilities with greater effectiveness. The handbook will build on your existing skills and show you how to compose commands that do more. You'll learn how to save time by issuing those commands more quickly, with less typing.

- *You've used only csh and are wondering about tcsh.* You'll find out about the latter's special features, and discover how *tcsh* builds on *csh*'s capabilities to provide a more productive working environment.

Scope of This Handbook

This handbook is divided into three parts. Part I, *Learning the Basics*, is designed to get you off the ground by providing a basic introduction to the shell and a broad survey that shows how to use the shell's more advanced features to accomplish many different kinds of tasks.

Part II, *Becoming More Efficient*, provides a more topical approach to the shell's capabilities. The chapters in Part II focus on particular aspects of the shell. You'll find these chapters useful when you want more information about features of the shell that are demonstrated in Part I.

Part III contains the appendixes, which provide information about obtaining and installing *tcsh*, a quick reference to those shell capabilities discussed in this handbook, and pointers to other documentation relating to *csh* and *tcsh*.

Part I, Learning the Basics

Chapter 1, *Introduction*, discusses the purpose of the shell and describes how to change your login shell to one of those discussed in this handbook.

Chapter 2, *A Shell Primer*, provides a summary of introductory essentials. If you already know something about running commands, you can skim this chapter as a review or skip it.

Chapter 3, *Using the Shell Effectively*, is an overview of many of the facilities that the shell provides to help you work more efficiently—easy, practical ways to get more out of the command line. Often, even experienced users are not aware of all of these features. This chapter gives you a glimpse of the kinds of techniques that are covered in detail in the rest of the book.

Part II, Becoming More Efficient

Chapter 4, *The Shell Startup Files*, describes `~/.cshrc` and `~/.login`, the files that the shell uses to initialize your working environment. This chapter also provides guidelines for modifying the startup files to suit your preferences.

Chapter 5, *Setting Up Your Terminal*, discusses how to find out what your terminal's special characters are (e.g., for backspacing) and how to change them if you don't like the default settings.

Chapter 6, *Using Your Command History*, discusses how to type less by using your command history.

Chapter 7, *The tcsh Command-Line Editor*, describes the facilities offered by the editor which enable you to edit commands interactively.

Chapter 8, *Using Aliases To Create Command Shortcuts*, discusses how to type less by using the shell's alias mechanism to create command shortcuts.

Chapter 9, *File-Naming Shortcuts*, describes ways in which the shell can supply filename arguments for you so that you don't have to type them all out yourself.

Chapter 10, *Filename and Programmed Completion*, describes how to use the shell for completing filenames after you type just the leading prefix. It also discusses how *tcsh* can complete other types of words besides filenames and how to set up programmed completions.

Chapter 11, *Quoting and Special Characters*, describes the shell's quoting rules. By following these rules, you can type any characters in a command line, even special ones, without having them misinterpreted.

Chapter 12, *Using Commands To Generate Arguments*, discusses command substitution, a facility that lets you construct pieces of a command line from the output of other commands.

Chapter 13, *Navigating the File System*, describes how to move around in the file system efficiently.

Chapter 14, *Keeping Track of Where You Are*, describes how to stay informed about your current location in the file system.

Chapter 15, *Job Control*, shows how to suspend, resume, and kill jobs; switch between jobs; and move jobs between the foreground and background.

Part III, Appendixes

Appendix A, *Obtaining and Installing tcsh*, describes how to make *tcsh* available on your system if you don't have the current version.

Appendix B, *csh and tcsh Quick Reference*, is a summary of those features and capabilities of *csh* and *tcsh* described in this handbook.

Appendix C, *Other Sources of Information*, contains pointers to other documentation. The most important of these references is the *tcsh* manual page. It's available in several forms, one of which can be navigated via hypertext links with a World Wide Web browser.

How To Read This Handbook

First, you should read Chapter 1. If necessary, change your login shell to *csh* or *tcsh*, using the instructions there.

If you're a beginner, unfamiliar with the shell, or just want to review the basics of executing simple commands, you should proceed to Chapter 2. If you're also having trouble figuring out how to do things like getting your terminal to backspace correctly, you may find it helpful to read Chapter 5.

If you already know something about the shell, you can skip the primer and proceed to Chapter 3. This chapter is designed to "jump start" you into better use of the shell by presenting lots of shortcuts that save you time and effort. You'll quickly become a more fluent command-line user by applying the information you find here.

For a more systematic and topical approach to the shell's capabilities, look at the chapters in Part II. They explain in greater detail the features of the shell that were briefly demonstrated in Chapter 3.

Finally, use the index. The shell's features interrelate, so you'll often find that a particular capability can be applied in many different contexts, and most likely will be discussed in several places.

Conventions Used in This Handbook

Certain special characters on your keyboard are represented in the text in upper-case `Constant Width`, (e.g., TAB for the "tab" key). Other special characters are RETURN (sometimes labeled ENTER), ESC (sometimes labeled ESCAPE), DEL (sometimes labeled DELETE or RUBOUT), and BACKSPACE (which is the same as CTRL-H). Control characters, which you enter by holding down the CTRL (or CTL, or CONTROL) key and typing another key, are represented as CTRL-X, where X is some letter. (You might need the SHIFT key for non-alphabetic characters. For instance, if @ is on the same key as 2, you might have to hold down SHIFT to type CTRL-@.)

This book uses the following typographical conventions:

Italic   Used for UNIX commands, filenames, and variables.

`Constant`   Used in examples to show the contents of files or the output from
`Width`   commands. `Constant Width` is also used to indicate commands
                   you type.

`Constant`   Used in examples to show interaction between you and the shell.
`Bold`   The text that you type is shown in **`Constant Bold`**. For example:

> `% ` **`chsh`**   Run the change-shell command
> `Old shell: /bin/csh`   *chsh* displays your current shell
> `New shell: `**`/bin/tcsh`**   Type in the shell you want to use instead

`Constant`   Used in examples to represent dummy parameters that should be
`Italic`   replaced with an actual value.

           Used to show the position of the cursor on a command line. For
                   example, the cursor is positioned on the asterisk in the following
                   command:

> `% ` **`sed -e 's/^ `**▮**`//' datafile`**

Box   Used in examples to show where you need to type a special char-
                   acter. In the following example, you type a CTRL-V and a TAB
                   between the quotes:

> `% ` **`grep "`** CTRL-V TAB **`" myfile`**

Comments and Corrections

If you have comments on this book, suggestions for improvement, or corrections, please contact me by sending electronic mail to *dubois@primate.wisc.edu*.

Acknowledgments

My thanks to Partha S. Banerjee, Scott Bolte, Paul Placeway, Dave Schweisguth, Tim P. Starrin, Kimmo Suominen, Paul A. Vixie, and Christos Zoulas for reviewing the manuscript. Reviewer comments materially improved the content of this handbook. Tim Starrin suggested the section on read-only shell variables and provided the text on which it was based.

The members of the *tcsh* developer's mailing list provided assistance by discussing and clarifying several issues that I found confusing while writing. Dave Schweisguth was especially helpful in this regard; as the main force behind the current version of the *tcsh* manual page, he's familiar with the difficulties of trying to explain *tcsh*'s features clearly.

Mary Kay Sherer cast her skeptical eye over my sometimes dubious prose, ferreting out and correcting many paraverbal constructions.

Adrian Nye served as general editor, but more than that, Adrian originated the idea for the book, then provided the guidance and encouragement that made it a reality. My thanks also to other O'Reilly staff, including Len Muellner, Norm Walsh, Sheryl Avruch, Kismet McDonough, Seth Maislin, Kiersten Nauman, Juliette Muellner, and Chris Reilley.

Finally, I appreciate the willingness of my wife, Karen, to accommodate the writing of another book, and for providing the occasional necessary reminder to let the keyboard cool off for a while. She also assisted the writing process by discussing with me the structure, approach, and content of the book. These thinking-out-loud sessions were invaluable in shaping *Using csh & tcsh* into its present form.

I

Learning the Basics

1

Introduction

When you log in to a UNIX system, you're typically greeted by some sort of banner message and a prompt such as % or $. The prompt indicates that you're talking to a shell—a command interpreter that provides you with an interface to the services UNIX offers. Why the name "shell"? Think of a shell as a wrapper around UNIX, insulating you from the need to know the underlying details of the operating system. Your shell helps you get your work done by reading the commands you type and passing the commands to the operating system for execution.

This handbook is about *csh*, a popular shell that is well suited for issuing commands, and *tcsh*, *csh*'s more powerful cousin. When you use a shell, the shell's capabilities and your ability to effectively employ them have a direct impact on the efficiency with which you work. This handbook helps you get more out of *csh* or *tcsh* by showing you what the shells can do and how to use their services in interesting and creative ways. Your shell will become more valuable to you, because you'll know how to use it to get your work done more easily.

Using the Examples

This handbook works best when read while sitting at the keyboard. Try the examples yourself (or make up your own commands based on them). In doing so, you'll more easily grasp the illustrated techniques. If I don't specify whether an example is specific to *csh* or *tcsh*, you can assume the example works for both shells. *tcsh*-specific features are noted as such.

It's likely that you'll need to make some substitutions in the example commands, due to differences among versions of UNIX. For instance, many of the examples use *more* to paginate command output, but some systems supply *pg* instead. Similarly, a number of examples use −*s* as the argument to the *mail* command for specifying a message subject, but on some systems *mailx* rather than *mail* understands −*s*. Printing commands vary quite a bit as well. I use *lpr* in the examples, but you'll need to substitute your local equivalent. Table 1–1 lists some of the substitute commands you can try.

Table 1–1: Command Equivalencies

If you don't have...	Try this instead...
more	*page, pg, less, most*
mail −s	*mailx −s, elm −s*
stty all	*stty −a*
lpr	*lp*
emacs	*gmacs, gnumacs*
colrm	*cut −c*

Selecting a Login Shell

Your login shell is the shell that the system starts up for you when you log in. You should determine which shell is your login shell, and change it if it's not the one you want to use. The SHELL environment variable usually contains the pathname of your login shell. You can display its value by using the *echo* command:

```
% echo $SHELL
```

The response from *echo* should be a pathname such as */bin/sh*, */bin/csh*, or */bin/ksh*. The last part of the path tells you which shell you're using. If the shell you want to use is already your login shell, you're all set.

If you decide to use a different login shell, you need to know where that shell is located. Use the *which* command to determine the shell's pathname:

```
% which tcsh
/bin/tcsh
```

In this example, *which* indicates that *tcsh* is installed in */bin/tcsh*. (The path might be different on your system.) Once you know the shell's pathname, run your system's "change shell" command (probably *chsh* or *passwd −s*). Suppose your current shell is *csh* but you want to use *tcsh* and know from using *which* that its pathname is */bin/tcsh*. Make *tcsh* your login shell like this:

```
% chsh                    Run the change-shell command
Old shell: /bin/csh       chsh displays your current shell
New shell: /bin/tcsh      Type in the pathname of the shell you want to use
```

Some versions of *chsh* display a list of shells from which you can choose. Others need to be invoked this way instead:

```
% chsh dubois /bin/tcsh
```

The first argument is your username (the name you use to log in) and the second is the path to the shell you want to use.

Systems based on 4.4BSD use *chpass* to change the shell:

    % chpass -s /bin/tcsh

If your shell-changing command fails, see your system administrator. Otherwise, log in again and you'll be talking to your new shell.

Trying a Shell Temporarily

If you're not sure you want to make a given shell your login shell, you can try it temporarily. Type the shell's name to start it up, issue the commands you wish to execute, then terminate the shell by typing *exit*. For example, to run a sample session of *tcsh*, use the following steps:

    % tcsh   Start *tcsh*
    % ...type other commands here...   Run some commands
    % exit   Terminate *tcsh* and return to your login shell

You'll get an error message if the shell can't be found:

    % tcsh
    tcsh: Command not found.

In this case, the shell might be unavailable on your machine or installed in a non-standard location. Check with your system administrator.

A Recommendation: Use tcsh, Not csh

csh is widely available, especially on Berkeley-derived UNIX systems, where it tends to be the standard user shell. *csh* is usually available on non-Berkeley varieties of UNIX as well, such as those derived from System V. *tcsh* isn't "officially" supplied by as many vendors as *csh*, but *tcsh* runs on many versions of UNIX and is available free over the Internet. If *tcsh* isn't provided on your system, see Appendix A, *Obtaining and Installing tcsh*, for instructions on making it available.

I recommend you make *tcsh* your login shell for daily work. *tcsh* is more powerful and convenient than *csh*, and can help you get your work done more effectively. Some of the advantages *tcsh* offers over *csh* are:

- A command-line editor.

- Better word completion facilities than *csh*; *tcsh* can complete command and variable names in addition to filenames and usernames. Also, individual commands can be programmed to complete in specific ways.

- Spelling correction.

- Better assistance for entering hard-to-type filenames.

- *rm* * detection to help prevent disastrous file removal errors.

- Better standardization. Vendors often tinker with the version of *csh* supplied on their systems. This means you may find that *csh* behavior varies from vendor to vendor. With *tcsh*, you can put the same version on all your machines.

- With *csh*, you generally need to wait for your vendor to get around to fixing bugs. With *tcsh*, bugs tend to get fixed quickly because there is an easy way to report them and an active *tcsh* developer's group that addresses them (see Appendix C, *Other Sources of Information*).

Before You Read Further

You may find it helpful to get an idea of how much you already know about the shell before you read the following chapters. Run the simple commands shown below and examine their output:

`% more ~/.cshrc ~/.login`	Display shell startup files
	(try *page* or *pg* if you don't have *more*)
`% stty all`	Display terminal settings
	(try *stty –a* if *stty all* doesn't work)
`% printenv`	Display environment variable values
`% set`	Display shell variable values
`% alias`	Display alias definitions
`% history`	Review your history

Does the output from these commands make sense to you, or does it look like gibberish? If the latter, that's fine—try to remember how strange some of the command results look now. As you read through this handbook, occasionally run the commands again. Their output should become more and more comprehensible and you'll get a good sense of what you're learning as recognizable landmarks begin to appear in this unfamiliar terrain.

2

A Shell Primer

This chapter provides a simple, quick introduction to the shell. You should read it if you're a newcomer to the shell and/or UNIX, or if you want a general review before reading the rest of this handbook.

If a command used here is unfamiliar to you, try the *man* command to read the relevant online manual page. For example, if you don't know what *wc* is when it appears in an example, you can find out that it's a word-counting program by using the following command:

```
% man wc
```

To read about the *man* command, use this command:

```
% man man
```

Another helpful reference is the O'Reilly & Associates handbook *UNIX in a Nutshell*.

Entering Commands

To enter a command, type it and press the RETURN key. Some commands are simple enough that you can run them by typing just their name. Here are a few:

```
% date          Display current date and time
% who           Show who is logged in
% ls            List contents of your current directory
% mail          Read your mail
% clear         Clear the screen
% logout        (or exit) Terminate your login session
```

You'll get an error message if the shell can't find a command (errors usually occur when the command is nonexistent or you spelled its name incorrectly):

```
% glarbl                              Nonexistent command
glarbl: Command not found.
% dtae                                Misspelling of date
dtae: Command not found.
```

If you notice a typing mistake before you press RETURN, you can backspace by using the BACKSPACE or DEL key (if one key doesn't work, try the other). To erase an entire line, try CTRL-U or CTRL-X. To erase only the last word, try CTRL-W. (If that doesn't work and you're using *tcsh*, try ESC DEL or ESC BACKSPACE.) If you issue a command, and then decide that you want to kill it before it's done executing, try CTRL-C.

Commands sometimes take additional information, such as processing options or the names of files to read. These additional pieces are called command arguments. Specify arguments after the command name, and separate multiple arguments with spaces. Examples are given below:

```
% ls -a                   List all files in directory, even normally invisible ones
% sort -r file            Sort file in reverse order
% mv file1 file2          Rename file1 to file2 (file1 becomes file2)
% cp file1 file2          Make copy of file1 named file2 (file1 stays as is)
% rm file1 file2          Remove file1 and file2
% mail christine          Send mail to christine
% cal 1752                Show calendar for the year 1752
% grep boa snakelist      Find instances of word boa in file snakelist
```

You can issue multiple commands on one line by separating the commands with semicolons:

```
% date ; who ; ls
```

Conversely, you can enter a single command on multiple lines by ending all the lines, except the last line, with a backslash. The backslash serves as a continuation character:

```
% more file1 file2 file3 \
file4 file5 file6 \
file7 file8
```

Command Input and Output

By default, most commands that produce output write to your terminal. If you use the > character, the shell lets you send the output to a file instead:

```
% who > users             Write user list to file named users
% cat file1 file2 > file3 Combine (concatenate) file1 and file2 into file3
```

This is known as output redirection. If the output file does not exist, it is created. If the file already exists, its contents are overwritten:

```
% sort data > junk          Sort data into junk
% cal 1995 > junk           Overwrite junk with 1995 calendar
```

Another form of output redirection uses the >> characters to append output to a file. You can record your disk usage as of a given date, like this:

```
% date > junk               Write date into junk
% du >> junk                Add disk space usage report to junk
```

When you write a command's output to a file, you can use it later in different ways without having to run the command over and over:

```
% who > users               Write user list to file named users
% more users                Look at user list
% wc -l users               Count number of lines (i.e., number of users)
% sort users > sorted-users Sort user list into another file
```

Many commands read from the terminal by default. That is, they read whatever you type until you enter a line consisting only of CTRL-D, which signifies end of file. For instance, to send a mail message, you can start up the mailer, type in your message, and then terminate the message with CTRL-D:

```
% mail javaman
How about joining us for lunch tomorrow?
(If you're not hungry, you can just drink coffee!)
CTRL-D
```

For such commands, the shell supports input redirection. If you have your mail message in a file named *my-msge*, you can redirect the input using the < character so that *mail* reads from the file instead of the terminal:

```
% mail javaman < my-msge
```

Input and output redirection can be used together:

```
% tr a-z A-Z < in > out     Translate lowercase to uppercase
```

Input redirection isn't used as frequently as output redirection. Input redirection is often unnecessary because most commands know how to read files that are named on the command line. For example, these commands have the same effect, so the < in the second command is just extra typing:

```
% sort data > junk
% sort < data > junk
```

Files and Directories

When you create a file, it's best to stick with "safe" characters in the name, such as letters, digits, and underscore. Periods and dashes are okay, too, but it's best not to use them as the first character of a filename. Letter case is significant in UNIX filenames, so *junk*, *Junk*, and *JUNK* refer to different files.

A directory is a special kind of file that's used to hold other files (including other directories). The directory in which you find yourself when you first log in is called your home directory. Directories help you organize your work because you can group sets of related files into separate directories. That way you don't need to keep everything in your home directory—a sure way to create an intractable mess.

Filename Patterns

When you want to specify several files on a command line, typing all the names explicitly quickly becomes annoying. Often, you can save keystrokes by using filename patterns. The shell interprets the patterns and finds matching filenames. Filename patterns are described briefly below. For more information, see Chapter 9, *File-Naming Shortcuts*.

The shell provides the following pattern-matching operators:

*   Match any string of characters. * by itself matches any filename; a* matches filenames beginning with a; *z matches filenames ending in z; a*z matches filenames beginning with a and ending in z; *a* matches filenames containing a anywhere in the filename.

?   Match any single character. ??? matches 3-character filenames; part? matches filenames beginning with part followed by any character; ?????* matches filenames that are at least five characters long.

[...]   Match any single character named between the brackets. [mM]* matches filenames beginning with m or M; *.[cho] matches filenames ending in .c, .h, or .o. A dash can be used to indicate a range of characters. For example, part[0-9] matches the ten filenames part0 through part9.

Filename patterns are powerful and help reduce typing, but they take a little getting used to. Use the *echo* command to practice using patterns. *echo* is safe because it does nothing but display the arguments that are passed to it by the shell. This allows you to preview a pattern's results without actually doing anything with the files named:

```
% echo [0-9]*                    What filenames begin with a digit?
00README
% echo *.ps                      What files are PostScript files?
fontlist.ps spiral.ps tiger.ps
% echo *.[ly]                    What files are lex or yacc source files?
parser.y scanner.l
```

"Invisible" Files

The *ls* command lists the files that are in a directory, but doesn't normally display dot files (those files whose names begin with a period). If you run *ls* after creating such a file, you won't see the filename—thus the file may seem as if it were never created! To see all files in a directory, use the *-a* ("show all") option. Try the following two commands in your home directory and observe the difference:

```
% ls                          List files, except dot files
% ls -a                       List all files
```

If you run *ls -a* in various directories, you'll notice that the filenames . and .. always appear. The filename . means "the current directory," and provides a convenient way to refer to your current location:

```
% chmod 700 .                 Make current directory private
% cp /usr/lib/aliases .       Copy a file to current directory
% find . -name core -print    Find core dumps under current directory
```

The filename .. always means "the parent of the current directory." .. is useful when you want to refer, or move, to locations one or more levels up in the file system:

```
% ls ..                       List the directory above the current one
% mv thisfile ..              Move a file from current directory to parent directory
% mv ../thatfile .            Move a file from parent directory to current directory
% cd ..                       Move up a level
% cd ../..                    Move up two levels
```

Creating Directories

Use the *mkdir* command to make a new directory. For example, to create a subdirectory named *NewDir* in your current directory, do this:

```
% mkdir NewDir
```

If you want the directory to be private, change its access mode:

```
% chmod 700 NewDir            Mode 700 = lock everybody else out
```

Changing Your Current Directory

The *cd* (change directory) command changes your current directory, that is, your location within the file system. With no accompanying argument, *cd* changes to your home directory, allowing you to return easily to "home base" from anywhere in the file system:

```
% cd
```

If you specify a directory, *cd* changes into it. The following are some standard idioms for moving around:

% **cd dir1**	Move down one level to *dir1*
% **cd dir1/dir2**	Move down two levels, through *dir1* to *dir2*
% **cd ..**	Move up one level to parent directory
% **cd ../..**	Move up two levels to parent of parent
% **cd ../dir3**	Move up a level, then back down to *dir3*
% **cd /**	Move to root directory (top of file system)
% **cd -**	Move to your last location (*tcsh* only)

Removing Directories

When you're done with a directory and want to remove it, use the *rmdir* command:

    % rmdir NewDir

rmdir fails if the directory is not empty (contains other files or directories):

    % rmdir NewDir
    rm: NewDir: Directory not empty

If *rmdir* fails and the directory appears to be empty, it may contain invisible files. Use *ls −a* to look for them:

    % ls -a NewDir

Ignore the . and .. entries, but if other files are present, remove them and then try *rmdir* again. Alternatively, you can remove a directory even if it's not empty using this command:

    % rm -r NewDir

The *−r* option tells *rm* to recursively remove *NewDir* and all files and directories under it. Yes, this option is dangerous! Think hard before you use *rm −r*.

Combining Commands

You can connect commands together with a | character (vertical bar, or pipe) to make the output of the first become the input of the second:

% **ls	wc -l**	Count number of files in current directory
% **who	grep colin**	Find out if *colin* is logged in

One of the most common uses of pipes is to add *more* to the end of a command so you can keep the output from scrolling off the screen:

% **cal 1492	more**	View calendar for year 1492 using pager

Commands connected with pipes form a longer command called a pipeline. Pipelines can consist of more than two programs. The following command lists the sizes (in disk blocks) and names of your files, strips off the initial "total size" line, sorts the rest of the sizes in reverse numeric order, and then displays the first five lines of the result. The effect is to report your five largest files:

```
% ls -s | tail +2 | sort -rn | head -5
```

By giving you the ability to construct pipelines, the shell allows you to do things that individual commands cannot do by themselves.

Pipelines and output redirection can be used together:

```
% ls -s | tail +2 | sort -rn | head -5 > big5
```

You can combine the output of sequential commands if you surround the sequence with parentheses. These two command lines are different:

```
% date ; who | more
% (date ; who) | more
```

The first sequence writes the output of *date* to the terminal and the output of *who* to *more*. The second sequence writes the output of both commands to *more*.

The same principle applies to output redirection:

```
% date ; du > junk
% (date ; du) > junk
```

The first sequence writes the output of *date* to the terminal and the output of *du* to the file *junk*. The second sequence writes the output of both commands to *junk*.

Running Commands in the Background

Normally, the shell waits for a command to complete before prompting you for another. If you think a command will take a long time to complete, and you want to continue working while it executes, you can run the command in the background. When you add a & character to a command, the shell starts the command in the background and immediately prompts you for another:

```
% sort huge-in > huge-out &
```

You can apply & to a command sequence to run the entire sequence in the background. The following command serves as a crude reminder to go home in 10 minutes:

```
% (sleep 600 ; echo TIME TO LEAVE) &
```

sleep pauses for the specified number of seconds and terminates, so the command waits 10 minutes and then echoes TIME TO LEAVE to your terminal. Since it runs in the background, you can continue to work in the meantime.

You can run multiple commands simultaneously in the background:

```
% sort huge-in.1 > huge-out.1 &
% sort huge-in.2 > huge-out.2 &
% sort huge-in.3 > huge-out.3 &
```

However, running lots of background jobs can result in high system load and slow response. If yours is a multiple user system, running a large number of background jobs could make other users unhappy, so be considerate and use moderation.

When Do Spaces Matter?

Command names and arguments are separated by spaces, but the number of spaces around a name and its arguments doesn't matter. These commands are equivalent:

```
% sort -r    file
% sort    -r file
%    sort -r file
```

In the commands shown thus far, I've usually put spaces around the following special characters:

```
; < > | ( ) &
```

Why did I insert the spaces? Simply, to make the commands easier to read. These characters don't require spaces around them, so the following commands are equivalent:

```
% ( date ; ls -s | tail +2 | sort -rn ) > sizes &
% (date;ls -s|tail +2|sort -rn)>sizes&
```

If an argument contains spaces, quote it to keep the shell from interpreting it as multiple arguments. For instance, when using *mail* to send someone a file, it's helpful to provide a subject using the −*s* option, so that the recipient can tell easily what the message is about. If the subject consists of several words, quote it:

```
% mail -s 'Here are the figures you requested' karen < budget
```

Without quotes, *mail* will think the subject is "Here" and the recipients are "are", "the", "figures", "you", "requested", and "karen".

You should also use quotes when a command argument contains other special characters, such as the parentheses and & in the following command:

```
% mail -s 'Playoff Schedule (for May. 6 & 7)' ian < playoffs
```

The Shell Startup Files

When you log in, the shell reads two startup files named *.cshrc* and *.login* from your home directory. If *.tcshrc* exists, *tcsh* reads *.tcshrc* instead of *.cshrc*. These files contain commands that set up your working environment—things like aliases, your terminal settings, your command-line prompt, and the set of directories your shell searches to find commands. You can edit the startup files to modify your environment; any changes take effect the next time you log in.

Become familiar with the contents of your startup files by running the following command in your home directory:

```
% more .cshrc .login
```

You might not understand everything you see, but the files will make more sense as you gain experience with the shell.

More information about the startup files, as well as guidelines for modifying the file, is provided in Chapter 4, *The Shell Startup Files*. Also, find *.cshrc* and *.login* in the index; this handbook presents many examples of startup file commands that you can use to customize your working environment.

3

Using the Shell Effectively

Chapter 2, *A Shell Primer*, introduced basic shell capabilities such as input/output redirection, filename patterns, pipelines, and background processing. These form the foundation of what the shell can do for you, but the shell has lots of other helpful features that users are frequently unaware of. If you learn some of these features, you'll use the command line more effectively and save time as you work. This chapter will teach you how to:

- Type filenames with less effort

- Repeat commands without retyping them

- Fix mistakes in your commands

- Refer to a file that has a space in its name or has a name that is hard to type

- Create shortcuts for frequently used command sequences

- Move around the file system quickly without typing long pathnames

- Suspend a command and resume it later

This chapter is relatively long, but individual sections are short, and show you quickly and without much reading how to use the shell more efficiently. Browse through the chapter and note the subject headings, then skip around as your interests dictate. When you want more information about a topic, turn to Part II, *Becoming More Efficient*. Check the index, too. Often, a given feature is discussed in several contexts.

Some of the techniques discussed in this chapter may seem strange to you at first. The best way to overcome this feeling is to try the techniques yourself. With a little practice, features that initially seemed odd will become second-nature, and you'll wish you'd learned to use them sooner.

Using Filenames

Most commands operate on files, so you frequently type filenames as you work. One way to refer to files quickly is to use filename patterns (introduced in Chapter 2, *A Shell Primer*, as a means of specifying groups of files). The shell has many other ways to type filenames with less time and effort:

- Filename completion, which lets you type a partial name and have the shell type the rest

- Spelling correction, to help fix typing mistakes

- Notation that lets you refer to your home directory easily

- Techniques for referring to a file that has special characters in its name (e.g., to rename it or get rid of it)

Letting the Shell Type Filenames for You

When you type the first part of a filename, the shell can often figure out the rest of the name, so that you don't have to type it yourself. This feature is called filename completion. To use it, you type the first part of a filename, hit a special key, and the shell types out the rest.

To trigger filename completion in *tcsh*, type a filename prefix and hit TAB. If you want to edit a file named *disestablishmentarianism*, type the first part of the name and let the shell finish the typing, as shown below (the ▮ indicates cursor placement):

```
% vi dis▮                        Type first part of the filename and hit TAB
% vi disestablishmentarianism▮   tcsh types the rest of the name for you
```

In *csh*, filename completion is used in a slightly different manner. You hit ESC instead of TAB, and, in addition, you must have the following command in your ~/.cshrc file:

```
set filec
```

If a prefix is ambiguous (matches more than one filename), the shell beeps; however, it still types out as much as it can—that is, as much as is common to all names matching the prefix. Type CTRL-D to have the shell list the matching filenames for you. This feature is helpful when you are trying to figure out how much more you have to type to make the prefix unambiguous.

If the cursor follows a space, the current filename prefix is empty. An empty prefix matches all names in the current directory, so typing CTRL-D after a space is a quick way of getting an *ls* listing while you're in the middle of typing a command.

To exclude filenames ending in certain suffixes from being considered for completion matching, set the *fignore* variable in your ~/.*cshrc* file to a list of the suffixes:[*]

```
set fignore = ( .o .bak )          Don't use .o or .bak files for matching
```

fignore is ignored if there is only one possible completion.

The shell has other completion capabilities in addition to those described above. To learn about them, see Chapter 10, *Filename and Programmed Completion*.

Using "Patterns" for Filenames that Don't Exist

Filename patterns using *, ?, or [...] are valuable for specifying groups of related filenames, but only if you want to refer to files that already exist. If you're trying to specify new filenames, you can use a different technique.

Suppose you want to create some directories named *Experiment1* through *Experiment4* to hold experimental data. A pattern like Experiment[1-4] doesn't work because the names don't exist:

```
% mkdir Experiment[1-4]
mkdir: No match.
```

Instead, use { } to specify the directory names:

```
% mkdir Experiment{1,2,3,4}
```

The shell looks at the comma-separated strings between the braces and generates one argument for each of them. The resulting command is equivalent to this:

```
% mkdir Experiment1 Experiment2 Experiment3 Experiment4
```

Using Shorthand for Home Directory Names

When you want to refer to your home directory or to that of someone else without typing out a long pathname, use ~ notation. A ~ by itself at the beginning of a pathname refers to your own home directory. This feature allows you to use that directory easily, regardless of your current location. For instance, if your home directory has a subdirectory named *Mail*, you can easily copy a file into it:

```
% cp myfile ~/Mail              Copy myfile to your Mail directory
```

Similarly, you can copy files from the *Mail* directory to your current directory, like this:

```
% cp ~/Mail/myfile .            Copy myfile from your Mail directory
```

---

[*] Parentheses are necessary when setting a variable to a value consisting of multiple strings.

Another form of ~ notation, ~*name*, means the home directory for user *name*. This notation can save you a lot of typing when you need to refer to locations in someone else's account. For example, if *alison*'s home directory is */usr/staff/alison*, the following commands are equivalent, but the second is easier to type:

```
% ls /usr/staff/alison
% ls ~alison
```

Not all accounts allow others to access them; messages like those below mean that *david* values his privacy and has restricted the access mode on his account to keep people from snooping around:

```
% cd ~david
/usr/staff/david: Permission denied.
% ls ~david
/usr/staff/david unreadable
```

You can make your own account private, if you like:

```
% chmod 700 ~
```

Because ~ is special only at the beginning of filenames, you can use the character as an ordinary character elsewhere within names. Some people like to use it at the end of a filename to signify that the file is a backup (similar to the way the *.bak* suffix is used):

```
% cp report report~          Make backup of report named report~
```

Letting the Shell Correct Your Spelling Mistakes

tcsh can perform spelling correction for you. This feature can be quite useful, especially if you're a poor typist. To turn on spelling correction, set the *correct* shell variable in your *~/.cshrc* file using one of the commands shown below:

```
set correct = cmd
set correct = all
```

The first form causes spelling correction for command names only. The second form causes spelling correction for the entire command line.

When *tcsh* thinks you've misspelled a word, it suggests a corrected command line:

```
% mroe myfile
CORRECT>more myfile (y|n|e|a)? ▮
```

Type y to accept the correction, n to refuse the correction (i.e., to run the command exactly as typed), e to edit the command, or a to abort the command. (To edit the command, you need to know how to use the *tcsh* command line editor. See "Reusing and Editing Commands" in this chapter, and Chapter 7, *The tcsh Command-Line Editor*, for more information.)

Be sure to look at the spelling correction that *tcsh* suggests—don't just type y automatically. This warning is especially true if you're creating a new file. The correction mechanism assumes the new filename must be wrong if the file doesn't exist, so it suggests one of the existing files, instead. This behavior sometimes leads the shell to propose corrections, like the one shown below:

```
% mv file1 file2
CORRECT>mv file1 file1 (y|n|e|a)? █
```

The suggested command is nonsense, so you should type n to run the command the way you typed it.

Dealing with Hard-To-Type Filenames

A file can be difficult to refer to if its name contains characters that the shell interprets in special ways. Suppose you have a file named *Preliminary Results* and you're trying to see what the file contains. You cannot simply type the filename, as shown below:

```
% more Preliminary Results
Preliminary: No such file or directory
Results: No such file or directory
```

The command fails because the filename contains a space. Spaces normally separate command arguments, so the shell passes two arguments to *more*, not one.

You can usually refer to such troublesome files by putting the name in quotes or by preceding each special character with a backslash to turn off any special meaning:

```
% more 'Preliminary Results'
% more Preliminary\ Results
```

In *tcsh*, it's often easiest simply to use filename completion to type messy names. When *tcsh* completes a filename, it puts a backslash in front of special characters to quote them:

```
% more Pre█                          Type filename prefix and hit TAB
% more Preliminary\ Results█          tcsh completes the name and escapes the space for you
```

See Chapter 11, *Quoting and Special Characters*, for general guidelines on dealing with special characters in filenames.

Reusing and Editing Commands

We've just seen some techniques for typing filenames easily. The following sections show how to use some of the other features that the shell provides for reducing typing: reusing and editing commands, using aliases to create command shortcuts, and command substitution.

The Shell's History List

The shell has a mechanism for maintaining a history list. That is, it remembers the commands you execute and allows you to rerun them with a few keystrokes. Suppose you're analyzing two data sets, reviewing the results of each analysis before printing the data:

```
% sed -e 's/^\(...\) *\([0-9][0-9]*\)/\2 \1/' data1 > temp
% anova Height Weight < temp | more
% anova Height Weight < temp | lpr
% sed -e 's/^\(...\) *\([0-9][0-9]*\)/\2 \1/' data2 > temp
% anova Height Weight < temp | more
% anova Height Weight < temp | lpr
```

There is a lot of redundancy in these commands. You can get the same results with less typing by reusing commands that you've already run:

```
% sed -e 's/^\(...\) *\([0-9][0-9]*\)/\2 \1/' data1 > temp
% anova Height Weight < !$ | more      Run anova, using temp as input file
% ^more^lpr                            Change more to lpr and rerun command
% !sed:s/data1/data2                   Rerun sed, changing data1 to data2
% !?more                               Rerun most recent command that contains more
% !?lpr                                Rerun most recent command that contains lpr
```

Before you try reusing commands, make sure that your shell is remembering them. Try the *history* command to display your history list:

```
% history
209   rm junk
210   pushd
211   ls
212   vi ch01
213   more appc
    ⋮
```

history should show your most recently executed commands, with a sequence number next to each one. Set the *history* shell variable, by putting the following in your *~/.cshrc* file. Change the number if you want the shell to remember more (or fewer) than the last 20 commands:

```
set history = 20
```

Once your shell is remembering commands, there are two ways to reuse them:

* First, both *csh* and *tcsh* provide a syntax that uses the ! character to signify references to commands in the history list.

* Second, *tcsh* provides a command-line editor that allows you to retrieve commands from the history list and rerun them.

Both methods of accessing the history list are described briefly in the next few sections. For more information, see Chapter 6, *Using Your Command History*, and Chapter 7.

The editor can use *emacs*-like or *vi*-like key bindings. In this chapter, I'm going to assume, for the sake of simplicity, that you're using the *emacs* bindings, which are the default at most sites. See Chapter 7 if you're interested in using the *vi* bindings instead.

Repeating Commands Using !-Specifiers

The ! character introduces a history reference, telling the shell to repeat something from the history list. The command-repeating specifiers are shown in Table 3–1.

Table 3–1: History Specifiers for Repeating Commands

Specifier	Description
!!	Repeat the previous command.
!*n*	Repeat command *n*, where *n* is the number shown next to the command in the output from *history*.
!-*n*	Repeat the *n*-th-to-last command, e.g., !-2 repeats the command before the last.
!*str*	Repeat the most recent command that begins with *str*, e.g., !ls repeats your last *ls* command. *str* need not be the full command name; it can be a prefix.
!?*str*	Repeat the most recent command that contains *str* anywhere in the command line.

When you use a history specifier in a command, the shell echoes the resulting command before executing it so you can see what it's doing:

```
% date                              Type a command
Fri Sep  9 13:38:43 CDT 1994
% !!                                Repeat it
date                                Shell echoes the command
Fri Sep  9 13:38:49 CDT 1994
```

Repeating Commands Using the Command Editor

In *tcsh* you can use the command editor to retrieve and execute commands. Type CTRL-P (previous command) and CTRL-N (next command) to move up and down through your history list one command at a time.[*] Each command is displayed as you retrieve it, with the cursor at the end. Hit RETURN to execute a displayed command. Type your interrupt character (usually CTRL-C) to cancel a command.

The simplest use of the command editor is a single CTRL-P to repeat the previous command. CTRL-P is equivalent to !!, but requires less typing.

---

[*] The up arrow and down arrow keys perform the same functions as CTRL-P and CTRL-N. You may find the arrows easier to remember.

To search your history list for commands that start with *str*, type *str*, and then
ESC p. For instance, you can type vi ESC p to retrieve the most recent *vi* command. If the command isn't the one you wanted, continue to type ESC p until you
retrieve the right command. (If you go too far, ESC n searches in the other direction.)

One advantage of the command editor over !-specifiers is that you get to see the
command you'll execute before you hit RETURN—no guessing is involved.

Repeating Part of a Command

It's often useful to repeat only part of a command rather than the whole thing.
You can use !-specifiers to do that. The !-specifiers shown in Table 3–2 are particularly helpful.

Table 3–2: History Designators for Repeating Words

Designator	Description
!*	Repeat all arguments from previous command
!^	Repeat first argument from previous command
!$	Repeat last argument from previous command

Use !* to copy all of one command's arguments to another command:

```
% grep Unix file1 file2 file3        Look for a string in some files
% grep -i !*                         Now do case-insensitive search
grep -i Unix file1 file2 file3
```

!$ is useful when you want to perform a set of operations on the same file:

```
% more document.ms                   Look at a file
% vi !$                              Edit the file
vi document.ms
% groff -ms !$ | lpr                 Format and print the file
groff -ms document.ms | lpr
```

Use !^ when you want only the first argument from the previous command:

```
% tbl final-report.ms | nroff -ms | more
% mail -s "Final report" june kokfung < !^
mail -s "Final report" june kokfung < final-report.ms
```

The shell provides other designators that allow you to repeat any word from any
command in your history list. These designators are described in Chapter 6.

You can repeat words using the *tcsh* command editor, too. Table 3–3 shows some
useful repeat commands.

Table 3–3: Command Editor Commands for Repeating Words

Command	Description
ESC _	Repeat last argument from previous command
ESC CTRL-_	Repeat previous word from current command
ESC /	Repeat most recent word from your history list that matches the word to the left of the cursor

ESC / is like filename completion, in a way. It "completes" the prefix to the left of the cursor, but looks for a match in your history list. If the match you find isn't the one you want, type ESC / again to search further back in the list.

Editing Commands

You can fix spelling mistakes or modify arguments with little typing by using the shell's ^^ mechanism:

```
% mre file1                     Run more to look at a file
mre: Command not found.         Oops!
% ^m^mo                         Change m to mo
more file1
% ^1^2                          Now look at file2
more file2
```

The strings that appear after the first and second ^ specify what you want to change and what to replace it with. The first string should not contain spaces.

^^ can be used to make changes only to your previous command. To perform substitutions on an arbitrary command from your history list, use :s// instead:

```
% !-2:s/abc/def                 Change abc to def in second-to-last command
% !nr:s/more/lpr                Change more to lpr in the last nroff command
```

In *tcsh*, you can also modify commands using the command editor. It's especially easy to change the last part of the command line, since that's where the cursor is located initially when the editor recalls a command. Erasing and retyping is often the easiest way to construct a new command from an old one:

```
% nroff -ms myfile | more        Run command
% nroff -ms myfile | more▮       Type CTRL-P to recall the command
% nroff -ms myfile | ▮           Backspace to erase more
% nroff -ms myfile | lpr▮        Type lpr
```

You can also erase and retype to fix a command that has a mistake at its end:

```
% nroff -ms myfile | moer        Run command
moer: Command not found.         Oops!
% nroff -ms myfile | moer▮       Type CTRL-P to recall the command
% nroff -ms myfile | mo▮         Backspace to erase er
% nroff -ms myfile | more▮       Type re
```

The command editor allows more general changes to be made (for instance, to add or delete words or characters anywhere within the line). See Chapter 7, for more information.

Repeating Commands Using a Loop

If you want to run a command once for each of a set of files, a *foreach* loop is often helpful. For example, if some files must be formatted and printed individually, you can use the following command loop:

```
% foreach f (intro.ms reference.ms tutorial.ms)
? gtbl $f | groff -ms | lpr
? end
```

After you type the *foreach* line, the shell changes the prompt as it collects the body of the loop. After you enter the *end* line, it executes the loop. Each time the shell passes through the loop, it sets the variable (*f* in this case) to the next word in the parenthesized list.

You can type more than one command between the *foreach* and *end* lines. Also, the words in parentheses need not be filenames. The example below uses the words as suffixes, to construct filenames in requests for *tcsh* mailing list archives:

```
% foreach suf (9311 9312 9401 9402 9403 9404)
? echo "Sending request for log$suf"
? echo "get tcsh log$suf" | mail listserv@mx.gw.com
? end
```

If you decide you don't want to execute the loop, type your interrupt character.

Creating Command Shortcuts

You probably have certain habits involving the commands you run. If so, you can save typing by using aliases—short names for often-used commands or command sequences. For instance, I use *more* and *history* a lot. By putting the following lines in my ˜/.cshrc file, I can run the commands more easily by typing *m* and *h*:

```
alias m more
alias h history
```

If you consider your own habits, you can probably think of some aliases that will help you enter commands more quickly. Suppose you often send files to your favorite printer with commands like these:

```
% pr file | lpr -Plwe
% pr -m list1 list2 | lpr -Plwe
% sort names | pr -5 | lpr -Plwe
```

An alias—let's call it *print*—allows you you do the same thing with less typing. Put this alias in your `~/.cshrc` file:

```
alias print 'pr \!* | lpr -Plwe'
```

Using the alias, you can type the previous set of printing commands like this:

```
% print file
% print -m list1 list2
% sort names | print -5
```

Notice that the definition of *print* is surrounded by quotes. That's because it contains special characters like | and !. The `\!*` in the definition expands to any specified arguments. (Arguments to an alias are normally tacked on to the end of the command the alias expands to. Using `\!*` allows you to place the arguments anywhere.)

Chapter 8, *Using Aliases To Create Command Shortcuts*, shows many more alias examples.

Using Command Substitution

Suppose you're working on a program and you decide to change the name of a variable from wdCnt to wordCount everywhere it's used. You can use the following command to identify which C source (`.c`) and header (`.h`) files reference the variable:[*]

```
% grep -l wdCnt *.[ch]
```

But instead of simply displaying the resulting filenames on the terminal, you can tell the shell to run the *grep* command and pass the names directly to the editor. To do so, simply put the command in backquotes:[†]

```
% vi `grep -l wdCnt *.[ch]`
```

The shell sees the backquotes and performs a command substitution: it replaces the *grep* command with its output (after changing newlines to spaces so the output becomes a single line). That way, you can edit the appropriate files without knowing which ones they are beforehand. If the *grep* command produces the filenames *defs.h*, *fileio.c*, *main.c*, *utils.c*, and *vars.c*, the *vi* command is equivalent to this:

```
% vi defs.h fileio.c main.c utils.c vars.c
```

Command substitution is useful in conjunction with other shell facilities such as command history. For example, you might run only the *grep* command to get an

---

[*] *grep* displays lines in files that match a pattern. *grep −l* displays only the names of the files that contain matching lines.

[†] A backquote is the ` character, not the ' character.

idea of which files contain the variable name, and then use ! ! to repeat it in the *vi* command:

```
% grep -l wdCnt *.[ch]
% vi `!!`
vi `grep -l wdCnt *.[ch]`
```

Command substitution is a technique that may, at first, seem esoteric and of limited use. However, it's such a useful method for constructing command lines that it should become an everyday part of your shell-using skills. See Chapter 12, *Using Commands To Generate Arguments*, for more examples and further discussion.

Navigating the File System

Unless you plan to do all your work in a single directory, you'll create directories in which to organize your files, and you'll move around between them according to what you're working on at the moment. The following sections describe how the shell makes it easier to perform repetitive location changes and to name directories into which you want to move. Chapter 13, *Navigating the File System*, provides more information about moving through the file system.

How To Bounce Easily Between Two Directories

When you need to run commands in two different directories, it's useful to know how to easily jump back and forth between them. *tcsh* lets you return to the last directory you were in, like this:

```
% cd -
```

Successive *cd* – commands flip between your current and previous directories.

Another method (that works for both *csh* and *tcsh*) uses the *pushd* command instead of *cd*. *pushd*, followed by a directory name argument, shoves your current directory to a memory stack, and then changes to the new directory. *pushd* with no argument exchanges your current location with the remembered one.

Suppose I want to alternate between ˜*/Database/Parts* and ˜*/Database/Suppliers*. I can do that the hard way, like this:

```
% cd ~/Database/Parts
% cd ../Suppliers
% cd ../Parts
% cd ../Suppliers
% cd ../Parts
etc.
```

pushd makes this job easier, as shown below. The first command changes the current directory to *~/Database/Parts*. The second command stores the current directory on the stack and changes to the *~/Database/Suppliers* directory:

```
% cd ~/Database/Parts
% pushd ../Suppliers
~/Database/Suppliers ~/Database/Parts
```

Now it's easy to move back and forth between the two directories:

```
% pushd                         Bounce back to ~/Database/Parts
~/Database/Parts ~/Database/Suppliers
% pushd                         Bounce back to ~/Database/Suppliers
~/Database/Suppliers ~/Database/Parts
% pushd                         Bounce back to ~/Database/Parts
~/Database/Parts ~/Database/Suppliers
etc.
```

pushd shows you which directories the shell remembers, displaying the current directory leftmost. This keeps you informed of your location as you move around. If you forget what's on the directory stack, use the *dirs* command. It displays the stack without changing your location.

popd removes the current directory from the stack and returns you to the location specified by the previous entry.

Letting the Shell Find Directories for You

To change into a directory, you usually have to specify a pathname. Suppose your account has the directory structure shown in Figure 3-1.

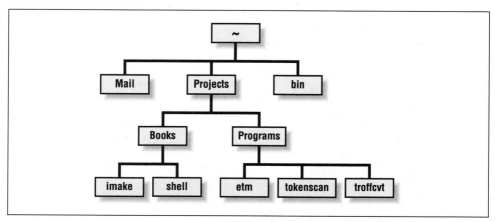

Figure 3-1: Simple directory tree

If you want to move in succession to the *tokenscan, shell, Mail,* and *Books* directories, you might use these commands:

```
% cd ~/Projects/Programs/tokenscan
% cd ~/Projects/Books/shell
% cd ~/Mail
% cd ~/Projects/Books
```

You can do the same thing more easily by giving the shell hints about finding directories. If you set the *cdpath* shell variable to a list of directories, the shell uses them as starting points when searching for directories when you use *cd.* This feature allows you to type shorter names as you move around. For example, you might set *cdpath* like this in your `~/.cshrc` file:

```
set cdpath = (~ ~/Projects ~/Projects/Books ~/Projects/Programs)
```

Then you can abbreviate the previous set of *cd* commands, as follows:

```
% cd tokenscan
% cd shell
% cd Mail
% cd Books
```

cdpath works for *pushd,* too.

Using Your Prompt

The default prompt string is usually % or >, which is pretty dull. This section illustrates some ways to make your prompt more informative.

You set your prompt by assigning a value to the *prompt* shell variable. The following command sets the prompt to the string Yeah?:

```
set prompt = "Yeah? "
```

The quotes prevent the shell from interpreting the ? as a filename pattern character and allow the trailing space to be included in the prompt.

It's best to experiment with *set prompt* commands from the command line. When you find a prompt that you like, put it in your `~/.cshrc` file, replacing any existing prompt setting. (You should also delete any *set prompt* command you find in your `~/.login` file.)

One simple way to make your prompt more useful is to include the current command number, by putting \! in the prompt string:

```
% set prompt = "\! -> "            Set prompt to command number followed by ->
44 -> echo hello
hello
45 -> date
Fri Apr 28 23:32:21 CDT 1995
46 ->
```

A prompt that includes the command number makes it easier to use !*n* to repeat commands that are still visible on your screen, because you can also see the command numbers.

Using tcsh Prompt Formatting Sequences

Interpreting \! in the prompt string is the only special thing that *csh* can do. *tcsh* can do that and more, using special formatting sequences in the string. Some of the possibilities are illustrated below. (The *tcsh* manual page lists all available sequences.)

Put a clock in your prompt

The sequence %t displays the time. %p displays the time, including seconds. (%T and %P are similar but use 24-hour format.) To display the day, month, or year, use %D, %W, or %y. For example:

```
set prompt = "[%W/%D/%y %P] % "
```

Make your prompt stand out

You can use %B, %U, or %S to turn on boldfacing, underlining, or standout mode (inverse video) in your prompt. Use %b, %u, or %s to turn these highlighting attributes off. For example:

```
set prompt = "%BYou rang?%b "        Use a boldface prompt
```

An emphasized prompt makes it easier to locate earlier command lines in a busy screen, particularly if you use a terminal window with scrollback capabilities.

Put your current location in your prompt

While you're actively working in a directory, it's usually not too difficult to remember where you are. However, if you leave your terminal for a while, or work in a multiple window environment that allows you to maintain several simultaneous logins, it's easy to lose track of your current location.

You can solve this problem by changing your prompt: use it to display your current directory and/or host name, and you can find out where you are at a glance. Here are some examples of what you can do:

- Display the full pathname of your current directory:

  ```
  set prompt = "%/% "
  ```

- Display your current directory, using ~ notation if possible:

  ```
  set prompt = "%~% "
  ```

  The advantage of using %~ over %/ in your prompt is that the former is shorter when you're in a directory under your own account (which is probably most of the time). This leaves you more room to type before you reach the right margin.

- Display both the host name and current directory:

      set prompt = "%m:%~% "

  If you want the full directory pathname, substitute `%/` for `%~`.

csh lets you put your current location in your prompt, but it's more difficult. The relevant commands are shown in Chapter 14, *Keeping Track of Where You Are*. That chapter also describes how you can put location information in window title-bars or icons, if you're using a window system.

Using Job Control

A job is any command you've started that has not completed. The shell provides a job control facility that lets you stop (suspend) commands temporarily and resume them later, or move commands back and forth between the foreground and the background.

Why Job Control Is Useful

Job control gives you a form of job multiplexing that lets you manage the execution of your commands and switch between jobs:

- You can move a slow foreground job to the background, and work on something else while the slow job runs. Suppose you're running a large *sort* command or a network file copy that takes longer than you expected. Rather than killing the command and rerunning it in the background (which wastes the time you've already spent), you can stop the command, resume it in the background, and work on other things while it finishes.

- You can put a command to sleep, then wake it up again when you're ready to continue. For instance, if you're editing a file and find you need to check some other files before proceeding, job control gives you an alternative to quitting the editor. Just suspend the editor and resume it later, after running the other commands. You'll be returned to the point where you left off—with no need to read the file back in and find your position again.

- You can kill a command, e.g., if it starts producing runaway output, or you decide that you simply don't want to let it finish.

Basic Job Control

Try the examples shown below to learn how job control works. Table 3–4 summarizes the commands we'll use. I assume that CTRL–Z and CTRL–C are your suspend and interrupt characters. (If you use different terminal settings, make the appropriate substitutions. See Chapter 5, *Setting Up Your Terminal*, for more information about terminal settings.)

The examples use *sleep* to demonstrate the effect of the job control commands. The *sleep* command is ideal for practicing job control because it has two valuable properties: you can define a time frame that allows you to manipulate the job, and *sleep* is harmless, since it doesn't affect any files.

Table 3-4: Basic Job Control Commands

Command	Effect of Command
CTRL-Z	Stop foreground job
CTRL-C	Interrupt (terminate) foreground job
fg	Bring stopped or background job to foreground
bg	Move stopped job to background
kill %	Kill (terminate) stopped or background job
stop %	Stop background job
jobs	Display current job list

Stopping a job

To stop a command that's running in the foreground, type CTRL-Z:

```
% sleep 1000          Start foreground job
CTRL-Z                Suspend job
Stopped               Shell reports that job is stopped
```

Moving a job to the background

bg moves a stopped job to the background, and starts it running again in the process:

```
% bg                  Put job in background
[1]  Running   sleep 1000 &     Shell reports job number and its new status
```

The shell echoes the command line of the job being put in the background (the & indicates background execution) along with the job number and the new status.

Bringing a job to the foreground

fg brings the current job to the foreground (*fg* works for stopped or background jobs). When you bring a job to the foreground, the shell echoes the job's command line:

```
% fg                  Bring job to the foreground
sleep 1000            Shell echoes command line
```

At this point, the *sleep* command is in the foreground. The shell will wait for the sleep command to finish before printing another prompt, unless you make another change to the job's status.

Killing a job

It will take a while for the *sleep 1000* command to finish, so terminate it by typing CTRL–C.

Another way to terminate a job is to stop it with CTRL–Z, and then use *kill*. To see how this process works, execute the following commands:

```
% sleep 1000              Start foreground job
CTRL-Z                    Suspend job
Stopped                   Shell reports that the job is stopped
% kill %                  Kill job
[1]  Terminated    sleep 1000    Shell reports that the job is terminated
```

CTRL–Z plus *kill* is useful when you run up against a program that catches CTRL–C to prevent interruptions. Unlike *fg* and *bg*, *kill* requires a job specifier argument. The % argument means "the current job." (If you have several jobs, it can be hard to tell which job is current; that's not a problem when there is only one job.)

kill works for background jobs, too:

```
% sleep 1000 &            Start background job
[1] 2948                  Shell reports the job number and process ID
% kill %                  Kill job
[1]  Terminated    sleep 1000    Shell reports that the job is terminated
```

If the shell doesn't print a message indicating that the job was killed, try this:

```
% kill -9 %
```

kill –9 sends an uncatchable kill signal to the job.

Stopping a background job

There are two ways to stop a background job. First, you can use the *stop* command. Like *kill*, *stop* requires an argument:

```
% sleep 1000 &            Start background job
[1] 2987                  Shell reports the job number and process ID
% stop %                  Stop background job
[1]  Suspended (signal)  sleep 1000    Shell reports that the job is stopped
```

Alternatively, you can use *fg* to bring a background job to the foreground, then suspend it with CTRL–Z. This usually involves less typing.

Dealing with Multiple Jobs

Suppose several jobs are stopped or in the background. Use the *jobs* command to display information about them. For example, in the course of retrieving and building a piece of software, I might build up a job list that looks like this:

```
% jobs
[1]     Stopped       ftp 144.92.43.19
[2]   - Stopped       vi README
[3]   + Stopped       vi reference.ms
[4]     Running       groff -ms reference.ms | lpr
[5]     Running       make >& make.out
```

The output displays the command line associated with each job, as well as the job number and status. Jobs 1, 2, and 3 are stopped and waiting to be restarted. Jobs 4 and 5 are running in the background.

The job control commands from the previous examples operated on the current job. Because only one job was running at a time in those examples, specifying the job wasn't a problem. If you have multiple jobs stopped or running in the background, the commands you use to manipulate them are the same (*fg*, *bg*, *kill*, and *stop*), but you often need to be more explicit about which job you want to refer to.

The examples below illustrate the various ways to specify jobs. They refer to the *jobs* output shown above.

Referring to the current job

Job specifiers begin with a % character. % by itself refers to the current job. As a rule of thumb, the current job is the one most recently stopped. If you're not sure which job is current, use *jobs* to find out. The current job will have a + next to the status column. In our sample *jobs* output, that's job 3, so the following commands would affect the second *vi* command:

```
% fg %
% bg %
% stop %
% kill %
```

Referring to jobs by number

You can refer to jobs by number. For example, %4 refers to job 4, the *groff* command, and %1 refers to job 1, the *ftp* command. If we decided to kill the former, and resume the latter in the foreground, we could use the following commands:

```
% kill %4
% fg %1
```

Referring to jobs by name

You can use a string to specify a job. `%str` indicates the job with the command
line beginning with *str*; `%?str` indicates the job with the command line that contains *str*:

`% fg %ftp`	Bring the *ftp* command to foreground
`% kill %gr`	Kill the *groff* job
`% fg %?REA`	Continue looking at the *README* file
`% stop %?out`	Stop the *make* command

If the shell responds with `No match` when you use a `%?str` job specifier, try
putting a backslash in front of the ? character:

```
% fg %\?REA
% stop %\?out
```

Job Control Shortcuts

To cut down on typing when using job control, remember the following shortcuts:

- A job specifier, used alone, is the same as *fg* followed by the specifier. The following pairs of commands are equivalent:

```
fg %          fg %3          fg %ftp        fg %?lpr
%             %3             %ftp           %?lpr
```

- A job specifier followed by & has the same effect as *bg*, followed by the specifier:

```
bg %          bg %3          bg %ftp        bg %?lpr
%&            %3&            %ftp&          %?lpr&
```

- If you frequently run multiple jobs, you'll probably use the *jobs* command a
  lot. Putting the following alias in your `~/.cshrc` file can make typing that command a little easier, since you'll only need to type *j*:

```
alias j jobs
```

What To Do When You See "There are stopped jobs"

When you use job control, it's easy to forget about a stopped job (or even to be
unaware you have one, if you hit CTRL-Z accidentally). When that happens and
you try to log out, the shell warns you that there are jobs you may want to attend
to:

```
% logout
There are stopped jobs.
```

When you see this message, you have a couple of options:

- Type *logout* again. The shell kills any outstanding stopped jobs and logs you out. (If you use *exit* or CTRL-D to log out, two *exit*'s or CTRL-D's in a row work, too.) However, take note: this method is dangerous unless you know which jobs are stopped. The stopped jobs could be editors with unsaved changes, mailers with unsent messages, etc.

- If you don't want the shell to kill your jobs, bring each stopped job into the foreground and finish running it. When you've disposed of your jobs, log out. This method is the safest option.

The shell doesn't warn you about background jobs—there is no reason to, because they continue to run after you log out.

II

Becoming More Efficient

4

The Shell
Startup Files

When you log in, your shell doesn't operate in a vacuum. Its behavior is affected by your working environment, which includes:

- Terminal settings, such as your backspace and line kill characters

- Variable values

- Aliases

- Key bindings for the command-line editor (*tcsh* only)

- Programmed completions (*tcsh* only)

All of the above are initialized in the shell startup files.

This chapter provides guidelines for modifying your startup files, explains how to set variables, and describes how to organize startup file contents. It's important to understand and know how to modify these files, since your working environment strongly influences how easily you get your work done. Much of the shell's power is tapped by using your startup files to set up your environment the way you like.

Startup and Shutdown Files

When you log in, your shell sets up its environment by reading two files named *.cshrc* and *.login* from your home directory. If the files exist, the shell executes their commands before displaying its first prompt.

tcsh reads startup files a little differently than *csh*. If you have a file named *.tcshrc* in your home directory, *tcsh* reads that instead of *.cshrc*. In order to avoid repeating a qualifying phrase throughout this handbook, it should be understood that references to *.cshrc* mean ".*tcshrc* if it exists and you're using *tcsh*, *.cshrc* otherwise." Any exceptions to this convention will be clear from the context.

In this chapter, I assume that you are in your home directory, and I refer to the startup files as *.cshrc* and *.login*. Elsewhere, I make no such assumption and refer to the files as ˜/.cshrc and ˜/.login, to indicate explicitly that they're located in your home directory.

Your shell might also read system-wide startup files before reading the startup files in your home directory. Not all versions of the shell read system-level files, and the names of the files vary from system to system (they might be named */etc/csh.cshrc* and */etc/csh.login*, for instance). System administrators sometimes use these files to standardize aspects of the working environment across accounts. You can either leave those settings in place, or use commands like *unset*, *unsetenv*, *unalias*, and *uncomplete* to remove them.

If a *.logout* file exists in your home directory, the shell reads commands from it when you log out. Your shell might also read a system-wide file such as */etc/csh.logout* before reading the one in your home directory. Like */etc/csh.cshrc* and */etc/csh.login*, */etc/csh.logout* can be used by system administrators.

Getting To Know .cshrc and .login

If you're not familiar with your *.cshrc* and *.login* files, you should run the *ls* command in your home directory to find out if they exist. Specify the *–a* ("show all") option since *ls* doesn't normally show dot files (files with names that begin with a period):

```
% ls -a
.               .cshrc      .mailrc     Letters     Papers      calendar    src
..              .exrc       .msgsrc     Mail        Projects    junk        tmpfile
.Xdefaults      .login      .plan       Misc        bin         mbox
```

If you don't have *.cshrc* and *.login* files, you can create them with any text editor, but it's likely that generic versions of *.cshrc* and *.login* were installed in your home directory when your account was created. The generic versions might look something like this:

```
% more .cshrc
if ($?prompt) then
    set prompt = "% "
    set history = 20
    set cdpath = ( ~ ~/Projects ~/Papers )
endif
alias h history
alias ll ls -l
alias print 'pr \!* | lpr'
set path = ( /bin /usr/bin /usr/ucb ~/bin . )
% more .login
tset -I -Q
stty erase ^h intr ^c
setenv TERM vt100
biff y
```

It's okay if you don't understand the contents of *.cshrc* and *.login* the first time you look at them, but you should strive to understand them eventually. If you see commands in your startup files that you're not familiar with, check for them in the index of this handbook, read their manual pages, or ask a knowledgeable user on your system about them. Also, it's a good idea to see how other people use their startup files. Ask more experienced users for copies of their files, and ask them to explain the parts that you don't understand. You may even decide to copy some of what you find into your own files.

Modifying .cshrc and .login

You can modify your working environment immediately by typing commands at the command line, but changes made that way disappear as soon as you log out. To make sure that a command is run each time you log in, add it to one of your shell's startup files using a text editor such as *vi* or *emacs*. The changes take effect the next time you log in.

Some guidelines for modifying your startup files are given below. Follow them to avoid making trips to your system administrator after you've messed up a startup file to the point where you can't log in:

- Before modifying a startup file, make a copy:

  ```
  % cp .cshrc cshrc.orig          (or)
  % cp .login login.orig
  ```

  That way, you can restore it later, if necessary:

  ```
  % cp cshrc.orig .cshrc          (or)
  % cp login.orig .login
  ```

- Before adding a command to a startup file, try it from the command line to make sure that it works.

- Make one change at a time. If you change several things at once and something goes wrong, you'll have a hard time tracking down the problem.

- The shell treats lines that begin with # as comments and ignores them. Use this feature to add comments that document your modifications. These comments will help you remember why you made your changes when you review your startup files later on.

- Don't blithely delete commands you don't understand; they might be important. If you want to see what happens when a particular command is not executed, turn it into a comment by putting a # in front of it. If, later on, you want to undo the change, just remove the #.

- After modifying a startup file, try it out. But don't do that by logging out and logging back in—establish a separate login session instead. That way, if there is a problem, you find out immediately, but you still have your original login session (running in your original environment), so that you can fix it. This is especially important if you introduce a serious error into a startup file that prevents further logins! You can use *rlogin* or *telnet* to log in again without terminating your current login session, pop up another *xterm* window (if you're using the X Window System), or even go to another terminal.

Verify that you can log in successfully and that your changes have the desired effect. If the shell seems to process only part of a startup file when you log in, be alert for error messages, and try to determine at what point in the execution of the file commands stop being processed. You will probably find a command with an error in it right before that point.

- Finally, as you gain experience modifying *.cshrc* and *.login*, you'll know when to ignore the preceding guidelines. For example, you may modify a startup file and feel confident it's error free. You can then use the *source* command to tell your current shell to reprocess it, rather than logging in again:

```
% source .cshrc              (or)
% source .login
```

Using Variables

Variables control shell behavior, including the prompt display, where to look for commands, and whether to maintain a history list. The shell understands two kinds of variables: shell variables and environment variables. In general, shell variables are used internally by the shell and affect its own operation, whereas environment variables are accessible to programs started from the shell. Appendix B, *csh and tcsh Quick Reference*, lists several useful variables of each type.

Variables can be set directly from the command line, but you'll usually set them in your startup files, either to override default values that the shell supplies, or to define variables that the shell leaves undefined.

Shell Variables

Use the *set* command to define shell variables. Some variables need no explicit value; they have an effect merely by existing:

```
set notify                   Turn on immediate notification of job completion
set ignoreeof                Disable logging out via CTRL-D
```

Other variables require a value:

```
set history = 20             Tell shell to remember the last 20 commands
set prompt = "% "            Define command line prompt
set fignore = (.o .bak)      Specify suffixes to ignore during filename completion
set term = vt100             Specify terminal type
```

Values that contain spaces or other special characters should be put in quotes, as in the *set prompt* command above. Values consisting of multiple strings must be surrounded with parentheses, as in the *set fignore* command.

You don't need to have spaces around the = separating the variable name from the value. If you do, there must be spaces on both sides:

```
set history= 20          Illegal
set history =20          Illegal
set history=20           Legal
set history = 20         Legal
```

I prefer to use spaces because I find *set* commands more readable that way.

Environment Variables

Use *setenv* to define environment variables:

```
setenv TERM vt100           Specify terminal type
setenv PAGER /usr/ucb/more  Specify preferred output pager
setenv EDITOR /usr/bin/emacs Specify preferred editor
```

Notice that, unlike *set*, *setenv* has no = between the variable name and its value.

Environment variables differ from shell variables in that, although their values are known by the shell, those values are also accessible to programs you run from the shell. (For example, if your mailer allows you to drop into an editor to edit a message, it might determine which editor to use by consulting the EDITOR environment variable.) Environment variable names are usually in uppercase type. Uppercase is not a requirement, but is a useful convention that helps distinguish environment variables from shell variables.

Examining and Using Variable Values

Use *set* or *setenv* with no argument to see the values of all your shell or environment variables:

```
% set              Display all shell variables
% setenv           Display all environment variables
```

Some systems have *env* or *printenv* commands that act like *setenv*.

A reference to a variable *name* is written $*name* or ${*name*}. You can examine individual variable values using *echo*:

```
% echo $TERM $path           Display terminal type and command search path
% echo ${TERM} ${path}       This is equivalent to the above command
```

If you try to use a variable that doesn't exist (i.e., has not been defined), the shell complains:

```
% echo $junk
junk: Undefined variable.
```

If a variable refers to a filename, you can apply one of the modifiers shown in Table 4–1 to extract different parts of the value. Modifiers are applied using the syntax $*name*:*m* or ${*name*:*m*}:

```
% set xyz = /etc/csh.cshrc
% echo root $xyz:r extension $xyz:e head $xyz:h tail $xyz:t
root /etc/csh extension cshrc head /etc tail csh.cshrc
% echo root ${xyz:r} extension ${xyz:e} head ${xyz:h} tail ${xyz:t}
root /etc/csh extension cshrc head /etc tail csh.cshrc
```

Table 4–1: Variable Modifiers

Modifier	Description
r	Root of value (everything but extension following dot)
e	Extension of value (suffix following dot)
h	Head of value (all but last pathname component)
t	Tail of value (last pathname component)

Turning Off Variables

If you want to turn off a shell or environment variable, use *unset* or *unsetenv*:

```
unset mail               Turn off notification of new mail
unsetenv DISPLAY         Turn off X display specification
```

Making tcsh Shell Variables Read-Only

In *tcsh*, a shell variable can be made read-only using *set −r*. A read-only variable cannot be modified with *set*, or removed with *unset*:

```
% set -r xyz
% set xyz
set: $xyz is read-only.
% unset xyz
unset: $xyz is read-only.
```

A system administrator can use read-only variables to place a non-modifiable variable in the working environment of all *tcsh* users. At a busy site where terminal lines and other resources are at a premium, the following line can be placed in a system-wide startup file to log out idle users after an hour of inactivity:

```
set -r autologout = 60            Log out idle users after 60 minutes
```

Paired Variables

Some shell variables have a corresponding environment variable, so that setting one member of the pair implicitly sets the other. For instance, you can use either of the following commands to specify your terminal type:

```
set term = vt100            This also sets the TERM environment variable
setenv TERM vt100           This also sets the term shell variable
```

path and *PATH* are another such pair, although their values are specified using different formats:

```
set path = (~/bin /usr/bin /bin /usr/ucb)
setenv PATH /usr/staff/dubois/bin:/usr/bin:/bin:/usr/ucb
```

When you set either *path* or *PATH*, the shell automatically converts the value to the format required by the other.

Organizing Your Startup Files

You need to choose which of the two startup files you want to put given commands in. When I suggest an addition to a startup file in this handbook, I indicate the preferred file to minimize confusion. If you're making your own additions, consider the issues below when deciding where a command belongs.

You may discover that a little rearrangement of your startup files is in order even if you've never altered them. The boilerplate startup files that vendors ship for use in creating new accounts often have commands in the wrong file. For instance, the *history* and *prompt* variables are sometimes set in *.login*, rather than in *.cshrc*.

Login Versus Non-Login Shells

The shell you get when you log in is (naturally) a login shell, and it reads both *.cshrc* and *.login*. There are also non-login shells, such as those that execute commands implemented as *csh* scripts, or those that execute !*command* shell escapes from programs like *mail*, *more*, or *vi*. Non-login shells read only *.cshrc*.

Consequently, if a command must be run for each shell that starts up, the command should usually appear in *.cshrc*. Commands that need to be run only at login should appear in *.login*. Examples of the latter include:

- Commands that affect your terminal settings, like *tset*, *reset*, and *stty*.

- Commands that set environment variables. (Non-login shells inherit environment variables from the login shell, so you need to set those variables only once, using *.login*, not *.cshrc*.)

- Commands like *biff*, which controls the announcement of new mail, or *mesg*, which determines whether other users can write to your terminal.

- Commands that produce output. For instance, some people like to execute *uptime* at login time to find out how busy the system is, *msgs −q* to see if there are new system messages, *who* to see who else is logged in, or *date* to display the current date and time.

Interactive Versus Non-Interactive Shells

A shell can be interactive or non-interactive. An interactive shell interacts with a user, who types commands. A non-interactive shell receives input from another source, such as a script file.

Interactive and non-interactive shells have somewhat different capabilities and behaviors. For example, only interactive shells print a prompt or allow you to use job control and command history. Commands that apply only to interactive shells, reducing start up time:

```
if ($?prompt) then
    set prompt = "% "
    set notify
    set history = 20
    set ignoreeof
      ⋮
endif
```

The *if*-statement tests whether the *prompt* variable has a value, to distinguish between interactive and non-interactive shells.[*] This test works because interactive shells give *prompt* a default value before reading any startup files, and non-interactive shells do not. Commands that are relevant only to interactive shells can be placed between the *if* and the *endif*, and non-interactive shells will ignore them.

Don't set your prompt until after you check its default value. If you include a *set prompt* command in your *.cshrc* file before the *if*-statement that tests whether the prompt is set, the test will always succeed whether or not the shell is interactive!

Using the source Command

If you put a lot of stuff in your startup files, they can get pretty long. One way to reduce clutter is to group similar commands into separate files, and then reference them using the *source* command. For example, you might put your aliases and command editor key bindings in the files *.aliases* and *.bindings*, in your home directory. You could then refer to the files in *.cshrc*, like this:

```
source ~/.aliases              Process alias definitions
source ~/.bindings             Process key bindings
```

---

[*] The space after the *if* should be included. Some versions of *csh* fail if it's not there.

Another advantage to this approach is that if you change one of the individual files, you can *source* it without having to reprocess your entire *.cshrc* file.

Protecting tcsh-Only Commands from csh

Even if *tcsh* is your login shell, *csh* may read your *.cshrc* file occasionally. Some programs are implemented as *csh* scripts, so *.cshrc* might be read when *csh* is invoked to execute the script. Therefore, you need to be careful about putting *tcsh*-specific commands in your *.cshrc* file. An error will occur if *csh* tries to execute *tcsh* commands like *bindkey* or *complete*.

You can avoid problems by using the following construct to protect *tcsh*-specific commands from *csh*. It relies on the fact that *tcsh* sets the *tcsh* variable before it reads any startup files and *csh* does not. The result is that *tcsh* executes the conditional block and *csh* ignores it:

```
if ($?tcsh) then
    bindkey -e
    complete cd 'p/1/d/'
        .
        .
        .
endif
```

Another approach is to use *.tcshrc* for *tcsh*, and *.cshrc* for *csh*. A simple way to create *.tcshrc* is to copy *.cshrc* and add any *tcsh*-specific commands. However, later changes may need to be made to both files. As an alternative, you can create a version of *.tcshrc* that, in effect, executes all the commands in *.cshrc*, and then executes certain *tcsh*-specific commands, too. The layout shown below accomplishes this task:

```
source ~/.cshrc              Get all the usual csh stuff from .cshrc
bindkey -e                   Now do tcsh-specific stuff
complete cd 'p/1/d/'
    .
    .
    .
```

The .logout File

If a *.logout* file exists in your home directory, the shell reads it when you log out. This file can be used to hold commands you want to execute when you're done working—like *clear*, to clear the screen.

.logout is not processed if you use the *login* command to log in again, without logging out first.

5

*Setting Up
Your Terminal*

You interact with the shell through your keyboard, so it's important to know which keys have special functions for controlling your terminal:[*]

- As you issue commands, you're bound to make typing mistakes. You can correct them by backspacing over characters or words and then retyping, or you can erase the entire line to start over.

- Sometimes, you'll want to move a slow-running command into the background so you can continue working, or kill a command that starts spewing out more output than you expected. These operations are done by typing special keys.

This chapter explains how to use the *stty* command to find out what your key settings are, and how to change them if you don't like them. Your terminal is a tool that you control—it shouldn't control you.

Identifying Your Terminal Settings

stty displays your current terminal settings. Its options vary from system to system, but at least one of the following command lines should produce output identifying several important terminal control functions and the characters you type to perform them:

```
% stty -a
% stty all
% stty everything
```

---

[*] By terminal, I mean a keyboard-display combination. The display could be the screen of a real terminal, an *xterm* window running under X, or a screen managed by a terminal emulation program, running on a microcomputer.

In the output, look for something like this:

```
erase kill werase rprnt flush lnext susp intr quit stop  eof
^?   ^U   ^W    ^R    ^O    ^V    ^Z   ^C   ^\   ^S/^Q ^D
```

Or like this:

```
intr = ^c; quit = ^\; erase = ^?; kill = ^u; eof = ^d; start = ^q;
stop = ^s; susp = ^z; rprnt = ^r; flush = ^o; werase = ^w; lnext = ^v;
```

The words erase, kill, etc., indicate terminal control functions. The ^c
sequences indicate the characters that perform the functions. For example, ^u and
^U represent CTRL-U, and ^? represents the DEL character.

What the Settings Mean

There are many special keys on your terminal; the most important are those that
perform the erase, kill, werase, rprnt, lnext, stop, start, intr, susp, and
eof functions.

Line Editing Settings

The erase, kill, werase, rprnt, and lnext characters let you do simple editing
of the current command line. (Some systems do not support werase or rprnt.) If
you use *tcsh*, you also have access to a built-in general purpose editor, described
in Chapter 7, *The tcsh Command-Line Editor*.

erase

> To backspace over the last character, type the erase character. Common
> erase characters are CTRL-H (also known as BACKSPACE) or DEL. Terminals
> vary in what they provide. There is often a BACKSPACE key that produces
> CTRL-H, and/or a DEL (or DELETE or RUBOUT) key that produces a DEL charac-
> ter. Some keyboards have only a BACKSPACE or DEL key, but allow you to pro-
> gram the key to produce the character you want.

kill

> The kill (line kill) character completely zaps the line you're typing so you
> can start over. Common kill character settings are CTRL-U or CTRL-X.

werase

> The werase (word erase) character erases the last word of your command line
> with one keystroke. When you need to erase several characters, using word
> erase is often faster than hitting the erase key over and over. The werase key
> is usually CTRL-W. (If you're using *tcsh*, CTRL-W might not do word erase. Try
> ESC DEL or ESC CTRL-H instead.)

rprnt

> The rprnt (reprint) character redisplays the command line you're
> typing—useful if output gets splattered into the middle of your command line
> (e.g., from a background process, or from line noise over a modem

connection). By reprinting the command line, you can see what you had typed. The `rprnt` character is usually CTRL-R.

If you are on a System V UNIX machine, don't be fooled by documentation that says this control function is named `reprint`. The *stty* command actually recognizes `rprnt`.

lnext

> The `lnext` (literal-next) character lets you type characters into the command line that would otherwise be interpreted immediately. For instance, in *tcsh*, TAB triggers filename completion. To type a literal TAB into a command, type the `lnext` character first. The `lnext` character is usually CTRL-V.

Process Control Settings

The `stop`, `start`, `intr`, `susp`, and `eof` characters allow you to control running processes.

stop, start

> The `stop` character stops output to your terminal until you type the `start` character. These characters help you control the flow of output to your terminal.[*] The `stop` and `start` characters are usually CTRL-S and CTRL-Q. Some terminals have a "scroll lock" key that alternately generates CTRL-S and CTRL-Q.

intr

> If you issue a command that takes too long to finish, or that runs away by producing too much output, you can usually kill it by interrupting it. The usual `intr` character is CTRL-C.
>
> If the command that you want to interrupt disables CTRL-C to make itself uninterruptible, try suspending the command with CTRL-Z. Then, kill it like this:

    % kill %   Try this first
    % kill -9 %   Try this if plain *kill* doesn't work

> The `kill` character is different than the *kill* command; the former erases your current command line, while the latter clobbers a running program.

susp

> If you want to move a command into the background (e.g., if it's taking a long time to finish), first suspend it by typing the `susp` character (usually CTRL-Z). Then, resume the command in the background like this:

    % bg

---

[*] A better alternative is to pipe command output through *more*.

eof

> The eof character signals end-of-file to the process currently reading the terminal. If this process is the shell, the shell terminates. The eof character is usually CTRL-D. To prevent CTRL-D from terminating your shell, set the *ignoreeof* variable in your `~/.cshrc` file:
>
>   set ignoreeof
>
> Then you'll need to type *exit* or *logout* explicitly.

Changing Your Terminal Settings

If you don't like your terminal's settings, use *stty* to change them:

    % **stty** *function char*

function is the control function name and **char** is the associated character. For example, the following command sets the interrupt character to CTRL-C:

    % **stty intr ^c**

You can use either ^c or ^C; *stty* understands them both to mean CTRL-C.

To make sure your terminal is set up properly each time you log in, put the appropriate *stty* commands in your `~/.login` file, following any *tset* or *reset* commands that might already be in the file. Remember to log in again so that your changes take effect. (For information about your `~/.login` file, see Chapter 4, *The Shell Startup Files.*)

The next two sections describe how to deal with some common problems involving the erase and line kill characters. If you think your terminal acts funny even after setting it up with *stty*, look at another user's `~/.login` file or take a look at the *stty* manual page. You might find something specific to your system that needs to be set.

Problems Typing the # and @ Characters

On many systems, # and @ are the default **erase** and **kill** characters. These choices come from the days of hardcopy terminals and are no longer useful. If your `~/.login` file doesn't set **erase** and **kill** to something else, you may have a hard time typing # and @. Set the **kill** character in your *.login* file as shown below; CTRL-U is a common choice:

    stty kill ^u

Set the **erase** character as described in the next section.

Getting Your Terminal To Backspace

Everybody makes mistakes while entering commands, so it's important to know how to erase typing errors. Usually, you would hit the BACKSPACE or DEL key. If you have trouble backspacing, it's probably because the system and you don't agree on what the erase character should be. If you see ^H when you try to erase characters, then your terminal is sending CTRL-H (another name for the BACKSPACE character). Add the following to your ~/.login file to tell the system to interpret CTRL-H as the erase character:

```
stty erase ^h              Set erase character to CTRL-H
```

If you see ^? when you try to erase, your terminal is sending DEL. Put the following in ~/.login, to tell the system to interpret DEL as the erase character:

```
stty erase '^?'            Set erase character to DEL
```

Note that ^? should be quoted as '^?' or ^\? to turn off the special meaning that the ? character has to the shell as a pattern matching operator.

Did Your Terminal Stop Working?

If your terminal seems to be locked, you may have inadvertently typed CTRL-S, which stops terminal output. To get it going again, type CTRL-Q. Even if CTRL-S wasn't the problem, CTRL-Q won't do any harm.

It's also possible for your terminal to become confused, even if it's normally set up correctly. This situation can occur for several reasons:

- You ran a program that set your terminal to a special mode, but crashed before resetting it.

- You tried to display a binary file or a directory:

```
% more core
% more /bin/cat
% more .
```

- You logged in over a noisy modem connection. Garbage characters generated on the line can have adverse effects.

If your terminal is left in an unusable state under these or similar circumstances, try the following remedies:

- First, try CTRL-Q, in case a stray CTRL-S was sent to your terminal.

- If that doesn't work, type CTRL-J reset CTRL-J. (If character echoing was turned off, you might not see anything as you type.) The *reset* command might at least get you to the point at which you can log out and then back in, to re-establish your normal working environment.

- Finally, try CTRL-C to interrupt your current job, or CTRL-Z to suspend the job so that you can use *kill* to kill it.

6

Using Your Command History

Shell users often type out, in full, every command they want to execute. This is inefficient and unnecessary, since the shell lets you maintain a history list and recall commands from the list to repeat them. That way, you can enter commands more quickly, with less typing. As an example, the following two sequences of commands are equivalent (they're from a session in which agenda items were edited and format-checked, and then mailed and printed). The difference between the sequences is that the first doesn't make use of the history mechanism, while the second does.

Sequence 1:

```
% tbl agenda-apr | nroff -ms
% tbl agenda-apr | nroff -ms | more
% vi agenda-apr
% tbl agenda-apr | nroff -ms > agenda-apr.txt
% mail -s 'Here is the April agenda' tom < agenda-apr.txt
% mail -s 'Here is the April agenda' marian < agenda-apr.txt
% lpr agenda-apr.txt
```

Sequence 2:

```
% tbl agenda-apr | nroff -ms
% !! | more
% vi !^
% tbl !$ | nroff -ms > !$.txt
% mail -s 'Here is the April agenda' tom < !$
% ^tom^marian
% lpr !$
```

You can see that the number of keystrokes is reduced considerably by reusing commands that have already been issued, in either their original or modified form. The second sequence may seem cryptic if you're not familiar with the shell's history mechanism, but don't let that scare you. History references aren't hard to use, and you'll get used to the syntax quickly. This chapter describes how to make sure that the shell remembers your commands, and how to recall and modify them using the history mechanism.

In *tcsh*, the command editor has access to your history list, too. The editor provides another method for retrieving and rerunning commands. To learn how to use this method—and you should—see Chapter 7, *The tcsh Command-Line Editor*.

The History List

To use the history mechanism, you must set the *history* shell variable. When *history* is set, the shell remembers your most recent commands in a history list so you can reuse them later. Add a line like the following to your ˜/.cshrc file, to keep a record of your last 20 commands:

```
set history = 20
```

You can use a value other than 20, if you like. If you have a *set history* command in your ˜/.login file, delete it, and put the command in your ˜/.cshrc file, instead.

Reviewing Your History

Each command you issue is an event that goes in your history list. To see what's in the list, use the *history* command. In *csh*, each output line displayed by *history* includes an event number and the command to which the event corresponds:

```
% history
683   cd ~/src/rtf
684   more Imakefile
685   make World >& make.world
686   more make.world
687   make clean
688   cd ..
689   tar cf rtf.tar rtf
690   gzip rtf.tar
691   ftp 144.92.43.19
692   uuencode rtf.tar.gz rtf.tar.gz > rtf.tar.gz.uu
693   mail -s 'New RTF distribution' rtf-list < rtf.tar.gz.uu
694   rm rtf.tar.gz*
etc.
```

In *tcsh*, history lines also include a time stamp.

Output from the *history* command grows quite long if you set the *history* variable to a large number. You can pipe the output through *more* or supply a numeric argument specifying how many lines to display:

```
% history | more            Display history using pager
% history 5                 Display last five commands
```

tcsh and most versions of *csh* understand both commands shown above. Some versions of *csh* botch one command or the other, in which case you'll need to use the one that works.

Using Commands from Your History

Use the ! character to begin a reference to an event in the history list. The shell sees the !, determines from the characters following it which event you want to use, performs a history substitution on the command line, and then executes the command. To keep you informed, the shell echoes the resulting command before executing it. Here's a simple example using !!, the "repeat previous command" operator:

```
% date              Type a command
Tue Mar  7 13:01:25 CST 1995    Output from the command
% !!                Repeat the command
date                Shell shows the resulting command
Tue Mar  7 13:01:32 CST 1995    Output from the command
```

The full syntax for a history reference looks like this:

```
!event:words:modifiers
```

That's a mouthful, but most of it is optional. In practice, history references tend to be simple, such as !! to repeat the previous command or !$ to repeat its last argument. Here's what the parts of a history reference mean:

event The event (command) you want to refer to.

words Which words to select from the command. *words* is optional; if missing, the entire command is selected.

modifiers How to modify the selected event or words. *modifiers* is optional; if missing, the event or words are recalled without change.

The following sections describe the parts of history references in more detail.

Event Specifiers

A history reference begins with a specifier indicating which event you're interested in. You can refer to events in several ways (see Table 6–1).

Table 6–1: History Event Specifiers

Specifier	Description
!!	Previous command
!n	Command n
!-n	n-th-to-last command
!str	Last command beginning with str
!?str?	Last command containing str
!#	The current command line typed so far

Examples of each of the history event specifiers are given below.

Recalling the Previous Command

The simplest history operator is !!, which repeats your most recent command. Suppose you're checking a printer queue occasionally, to see if a print job is done. Type the queue-checking command once, then use !! to repeat it:

```
% lpq -Plwb
% !!
lpq -Plwb
% !!
lpq -Plwb
% etc.
```

Referring to Commands by Number

If you know a command's event number, you can refer to it using that number. For example, !12 repeats command 12. If you don't know the event number, run the *history* command to review your history list. To reduce the burden on your memory and lessen the need to run *history*, you can arrange to display event numbers in your prompt. For example, you can set your prompt in *˜.cshrc* as shown below:

```
set prompt = "\! % "
```

The shell expands \! to the current event number each time it displays the prompt. This feature lets you see at a glance the event numbers for any recent commands still on your screen, so you can recall them more easily.

Events can be specified by their position relative to the current command. !-2 refers to the second-to-last command, !-3 refers to the third-to-last, and so forth. (!-1 is acceptable, but !! is equivalent to it and easier to type.)

If I edit a file and send it to *cindy*, then realize I need to make another change, I can re-edit the file, notify her that another copy is on the way, and send the file again, like this:

```
% vi schedule                    Edit a file
% mail cindy < schedule          Mail it
% !-2                            Edit the file again
vi schedule
% mail -s 'I goofed' cindy       Tell cindy another copy is on the way
That copy of the schedule was
bad.   Toss it; I'll send another.
CTRL-D
% !-3                            Mail the file again
mail cindy < schedule
```

Since `!-`*n* notation is relative, it allows you to easily execute a set of events repeatedly. The following example uses `!-2` to alternate between editing and formatting commands:

```
% vi doc.ms                      Edit document
% nroff -ms doc.ms | more        Check whether or not it formats properly
% !-2                            Repeat the editing command
vi doc.ms
% !-2                            Repeat the formatting command
nroff -ms doc.ms | more
% !-2                            Repeat the editing command
vi doc.ms
% !-2                            Repeat the formatting command
nroff -ms doc.ms | more
etc.
```

Referring to Events by Command Name or Substring

You can refer to events with strings instead of numbers, and the shell will search backward through your history list to find the command you specify. `!`*str* repeats the most recent command that begins with *str*. `!?`*str*`?` repeats the most recent command that contains *str*. If the second `?` would be the last character of the command line, you can omit it.

Suppose the last part of your history looks like this:

```
347  who
348  wc -l data
349  cal 1776
350  emacs calendar
```

In this case, `!w` repeats the *wc* command and `!wh` repeats *who*. `!ca` repeats *cal*, but `!?ca` repeats the *emacs* command, since that's the most recent command containing ca.

The `!?`*str* form is often the easiest way to select a command that differs from others only in the text at the end of the line (like a filename). You usually know what filename you want to use, but not necessarily the event number of the command that used that filename.

Referring to the Current Event

!# refers to the current event—it means "everything you've typed on the command line so far." !# is used primarily in conjunction with word designators that select earlier parts of the current command line, so discussion of !# is deferred until the section "Repeating Words from the Current Command," which appears later in this chapter.

Erroneous History References

If you type a history reference that the shell doesn't understand, it complains:

```
% !xyz
xyz: Event not found.
```

Such a response usually means the reference is malformed or that the command you want to recall is too old and has been shifted out of the history list by more recent commands.

Adding Text to Recalled Events

When you recall a command, you can add new text to it, forming a new command:

```
% sort mydata | uni        Look at unique lines in sorted output
uni: Command not found      Oops, mistyped uniq
% !!q                       Add q to uni
sort mydata | uniq
% !! -d                     Now add -d to look at lines that are duplicated
sort mydata | uniq -d
```

Or suppose you run *diff* to compare two files, but the output scrolls off the screen because the differences are more extensive than you expected. Repeat the command and add a pipe to route the output through a pager, as shown below:

```
% diff prog.c~ prog.c       Compare previous and current versions of prog.c
% !! | more                 Try again, using more
diff prog.c~ prog.c | more
```

If you run a command, then decide you want to rerun it and save the output, you can add output redirection instead of a pipe:

```
% nroff -ms document.ms     Run formatter
% !! > document.txt         Repeat, saving output
nroff -ms document.ms > document.txt
```

The examples shown above add text to the ends of commands. You can also add text to the beginning of a command, as shown below:

```
% uptime                          Check status of local machine
% r!!                             Check status of machines on local network
ruptime
```

Resolving ambiguous additions

Sometimes, adding text to a history reference creates a new reference that doesn't do what you want. For instance, if you want to look at *data*, then *data2*, the following reference doesn't work:

```
% more data                       Look at data
% !m2                             Try to look at data2 using !m and adding 2
m2: Event not found.
```

For cases like this, insulate the reference from the following text using braces, as shown below:

```
% more data
% !{m}2
more data2
```

Word Designators

Commands consist of words. A word is a command name, an argument, an operator, or a special character like ; or &. If I type the following command:

```
% grep "Baton Rouge" addresses|sort>output&
```

the shell breaks the command into words, and numbers them as follows:

```
0      1              2          3  4    5  6      7
grep   "Baton Rouge"  addresses  |  sort >  output &
```

Words are numbered, starting with 0, so the command name is usually word 0, and the first argument is usually word 1.

The history mechanism allows you to reference any word from any command in your history list, using word designators. Most often, however, you'll probably want to repeat words from your previous command, using the designators shown in Table 6-2.

Table 6–2: History Reference Word Designators for Previous Command

Designator	Description
!*	Repeat all arguments from previous command
!^	Repeat first argument from previous command
!$	Repeat last argument from previous command

!* is useful when you want to run a command on the files you used in your previous command:

```
% more file1 file2 file3        Look at some files
% pr !* | lpr                   Print the same files
pr file1 file2 file3 | lpr
```

Or if you want to rerun a command, with an extra flag between the command name and the arguments:

```
% grep error file1 file2        Search for a word
% grep -i !*                    Do a case-insensitive search instead
grep -i error file1 file2
```

Using !$ to repeat the last argument is useful for doing a series of operations on the same file. To review, edit, print, and mail a file, you might do something like this:

```
% more checklist
% vi !$
vi checklist
% lpr !$
lpr checklist
% mail -s '!$ enclosed' dave < !$
mail -s 'checklist enclosed' dave < checklist
```

!^ is handy for repeating the previous command's first argument:

```
% pr myfile | lpr
% vi !^
vi myfile
```

The general syntax for repeating words from a command looks like this:

!event:words

In this syntax, *event* designates which event to recall and *:words* identifies the words you want from the event. Table 6–3 lists the various forms that *words* can take. Some examples of how to use these forms are given below:

```
!vi:*          All arguments of last vi command
!-2:$          Last argument of 2nd-to-last command
!?edu?:^       First argument of last command containing edu
!!:2-4         Arguments 2 through 4 of previous command
```

Table 6-3: History Reference Word Designators

Designator	Description
0	Word 0 (the command name)
n	Word *n* (argument *n*)
^	Word 1
$	Last word
m-n	Words *m* through *n*
-n	Words 0 through *n*
m-	Words *m* through (but not including) last word
-	Words 0 through (but not including) last word
*m**	Words *m* through last word
*	Words 1 through last word, or empty if there are no arguments
%	Following a !?*str*? event specifier, the word matched by *str*

Word Designator Shorthand

You can sometimes abbreviate word designators, using the following rules:

- If you're applying a designator to the previous command, you can shorten the event reference from !! to !. For example, !!:0 and !:0 are equivalent, as are !!:2-4 and !:2-4.

- When a designator begins with ^, $, *, or %, you can omit the preceding colon.

After considering these rules, you can see the origins of !*, !^, and !$: they're actually the shorthand forms of !!:*, !!:^, and !!:$. For instance, !!:* becomes !:* by the first rule, and !* by the second.

According to the *csh* manual page, you can drop the colon preceding word designators that begin with -, but it's better not to. For example, !:-3 becomes !-3 that way, but !:-3 (words 0 through 3 of the previous command) is a history reference with an entirely different meaning than !-3 (third-to-last command). Similarly, !:- becomes !- when you drop the colon. However, many versions of the shell choke on !-.

Using Word Designators

History event specifiers sometimes look a bit odd, and can look even more so when you start adding word designators to them. Thus, it's understandable if you're initially skeptical about whether word designators are really very useful or easy to learn. In fact, they are both, and when you actually start typing word designators yourself, you'll find that you get used to them fairly quickly.

!*, !^, and !$ are the easiest designators to use and remember, and the following sections describe some practical uses for a few of the others. To become accustomed to using designators in your own work, be alert for situations in which you plan to use arguments that were recently used in other commands. A good rule of thumb is that when you need to repeat a series of arguments or long arguments like full pathnames, you can probably use word designators to good effect.

Repeating a Set of Words

The *m–n* range designator lets you specify any set of contiguous words:

```
% grep history ch00 ch06 appb
% vi !:2-4
vi ch00 ch06 appb
```

You can omit *m*, *n*, or both from a range designator. If *m* is omitted, the range begins with word 0. If *n* is omitted, the range ends with the word before the last. Thus, !:- is a quick way to repeat everything but the last word of a command. This method is useful if you want to supply a different last word, as shown below:

```
% nroff -ms intro.ms | more          Format and view a document
% !:- lpr                            Now send it to the printer
nroff -ms intro.ms | lpr
% grep -i trials method.ms           Search a file for a string
% !:- results.ms                     Search a different file for the same string
grep -i trials results.ms
```

m-$ is a legal range designator (word *m* through the last word), but *m** means the same thing and is easier to type.

Repeating Words from the Current Command

!# refers to everything that appears to the left of itself on the current command line. Therefore, you can often construct a new argument from an argument you've already typed, by using !# and a word designator. For instance, you can easily make a backup copy of a file by using !#^ to repeat the first argument of the current command:

```
% cp observations !#^.bak
```

The most common word designators using !# are listed in Table 6–4.

Table 6–4: Word Designators for the Current Command

Designator	Description
!#*	All arguments
!#^	First argument
!#$	Last argument
!#:n	Argument n

!# is most useful for arguments that resemble each other. The following pairs of commands are equivalent, but the second member of each pair uses !# to save typing:

```
% gtbl ref-manual | groff -ms > ref-manual.ps
% gtbl ref-manual | groff -ms > !#^.ps

% diff Instructions Instructions.old
% diff Instructions !#^.old
```

Event Modifiers

Following a word designator (or an event specifier if there is no designator) you can add an event modifier:

```
!event:words:modifiers
!event:modifiers
```

Modifiers change the way an event is treated. If you add :p to an event reference, the event is printed (echoed) but not executed. Other modifiers change the text of the recalled event or words in some way. For instance, adding :s/a/b changes a to b in the command line. This feature is useful for fixing mistakes or modifying an argument. Possible modifiers are listed in Table 6–5.

Table 6–5: History Reference Modifiers

Modifier	Description
p	Print resulting command without executing it
s/*old*/*new*/	Perform substitution, replacing *old* with *new*
&	Repeat previous s substitution
r	Root of filename (everything but extension following dot)
e	Extension of filename (suffix following dot)
h	Head of pathname (all but last component)
t	Tail of pathname (last component)
q	Quote words (prevents filename pattern expansion)
x	Like q but break into words at whitespace
u	Make first lowercase letter uppercase (*tcsh* only)
l	Make first uppercase letter lowercase (*tcsh* only)
g	Apply modifier following g globally to each word
a	Apply modifier(s) following a as many times as possible to a word. If used with g, a is applied to all words. (*tcsh* only)

Modifiers vary a great deal in terms of their general usefulness. I find that :s and :p are the most valuable. The following sections discuss :p, the substitution modifier :s (along with the repetition modifiers :g, :a, and :&), and the filename modifiers :r, :e, :h, and :t.

Recalling Commands Without Executing Them

`:p` causes an event to be echoed but not executed. This feature is useful if you're unsure whether a reference specifies the command you want. When you've found the right one, use `!!` to repeat it:

```
% !r:p                              Recall last rlogin command without executing it
rm *.ps                             Oops, that's not it!
% !rl:p                             Try again, specifying more of the command name
rlogin ruby.ora.com -l dubois       Yes, that's the one
% !!                                Execute it
rlogin ruby.ora.com -l dubois
```

Judicious use of `:p` can help you avoid problems. If you had typed the first `!r` in the preceding example without the `:p`, you'd execute the *rm* command again. That might not be a good idea. (If you had moved into another directory after you originally executed the *rm* command, you might remove files that you want to keep.)

Substitution Modifiers

The shell's history mechanism supports a simple form of command editing, which uses the `:s/old/new/` modifier. *old* is the string to change and *new* is what to replace it with. For instance, I can format a file to the screen, and then to the printer, like this:

```
% tbl Install-instructions | nroff -ms | more
% !:s/more/lpr/
tbl Install-instructions | nroff -ms | lpr
```

The effect of the `:s` modifier is similar to the `s` substitution command in *sed* or *ex*, although there are some differences. For example, *old* is a literal string, not a pattern, and most versions of the shell do not allow *old* to contain spaces.

The shorthand form `^old^new^` changes *old* to *new* in the previous command, as shown below:

```
% more Install-instructions
% ^more^vi^
vi Install-instructions
```

The `^old^new` form is easier to type, but it allows you to modify only the most recent command. The `:s/old/new` form is longer, but more general. It can be used with any command from your history list. For both forms, if the final delimiter (/ or ^) would be the last character on the command line, you can omit it.

^old^new has many uses:

- To fix small mistakes in a command:

```
% cd porgrams                    Change into programs directory
programs: No such directory.     Oops!
% ^or^ro                         Change or to ro
cd programs
```

- To repeat an operation on successive files:

```
% nroff -ms file1 | lpr          Format and print file1
% ^1^2                           Do same with file2
nroff -ms file2 | lpr
% ^2^3                           Do same with file3
nroff -ms file3 | lpr
```

- To change the options to a command:

```
% ls -l /usr/spool/mqueue        Generate long listing
% ^-l^-lt                        Sort listing by file modification times
ls -lt /usr/spool/mqueue

% grep -i internet file          Do a case-insensitive search
% ^i^ni                          Add line numbers to output
grep -ni internet file
```

Be sure that *old* provides enough context to specify unambiguously what you want to modify. Otherwise, you might change the wrong thing:

```
% sort data-a                    Sort data-a
% ^a^b                           Now sort data-b
sort dbta-a                      Oops, changed the wrong a (should have used ^-a^-b)
sort: can't open dbta-a: No such file or directory
```

:s/old/new can do anything that *^old^new* can, albeit with a little more typing. And since you use *:s* with an event specifier, you can use it to modify any command in your history list, not just the most recent one:

```
% vi myfile.ms                   Edit a file
% nroff -ms myfile.ms | more     Format it and view the output
% !vi:s/e/e2                     Change myfile.ms to myfile2.ms in vi command
vi myfile2.ms
% !-2:s/more/lpr                 Change more to lpr in second-to-last command
nroff -ms myfile.ms | lpr
```

Keep in mind the following properties of the *:s* modifier so that you can exploit its capabilities to full effect:

- & placed anywhere in *new* expands to *old*. Thus, *:s/junk/&yard* is equivalent to *:s/junk/junkyard*. To use a & literally, put a \ in front of it.

- The delimiter character need not be /. You can use any character. This is convenient if / appears in *old* or *new*:

```
% lynx http:/www.whitehouse.gov/
Unable to access remote host
% !:s#/#//
lynx http://www.whitehouse.gov/
```

    Alternatively, \ may be used to quote / within either string. This can get ugly, though:

```
% lynx http:/www.whitehouse.gov/
Unable to access remote host
% !:s/\//\/\/ .
lynx http://www.whitehouse.gov/
```

- If *old* is empty, its value is taken from the *old* in the previous use of :s or from the *str* in the previous use of the !?*str*? event specifier, whichever occurred most recently.

- If *new* is empty and there is nothing else on the command line, you can also omit the second delimiter. This form deletes the characters in *new*:[*]

```
% more superfluous
% !:s/fluous
more super
```

- You can apply :s to an individual word.[†] The following command uses !#^ to duplicate the first word of the current command line and :s to modify the duplicate:

```
% mv AllocColor.c !#^:s/A/XA
mv AllocColor.c XAllocColor.c
```

Repeating a substitution

The :s modifier changes only the first instance of *old* in the selected command or words:

```
% echo a a a a
a a a a
% !:s/a/b
echo b a a a
b a a a
% echo !:2-3:s/a/b
echo b a
b a
```

---

* Some versions of *csh* may not allow this.
† Some versions of *csh* may not allow this.

To make the substitution in all words that contain *old*, use :gs instead. The following sequence encodes and mails two files. The filename argument needs to be changed globally because it appears more than once in each command:

```
% uuencode file1 file1 > file1.uu            Encode the first file
% !:gs/1/2                                   Encode the second file
uuencode file2 file2 > file2.uu
% mail -s 'Here is file1' boss < file1.uu    Mail the first file
% !:gs/1/2                                    Mail the second file
mail -s 'Here is file2' boss < file2.uu
```

Although :gs performs the substitution in each word of a command, it changes *old* only once in each word, even if it occurs multiple times in a word:

```
% echo abc abcabc
% !:gs/abc/def
echo def defabc
```

In *tcsh*, you can cause the substitution to take place as many times as possible by adding a to the :gs modifier:

```
% echo abc abcabc
% !:ags/abc/def
echo def defdef
```

Be careful, though—a modifier like :as/x/xx causes a substitution loop, as shown below:

```
% echo x
x
% !:as/x/xx
Substitution buffer overflow.
```

Repeating the previous substitution

:& repeats the previous :s/*old*/*new* or ^*old*^*new* substitution.

```
% grep -i expenditure file1     Look for string in file1
% !:s/e1/e2                     Look for the same string in file2
grep -i expenditure file2
% pr file1 | lpr                Print file1
% !:&                           Repeat substitution to print file2
pr file2 | lpr
```

:g& repeats the previous substitution globally.

Checking a substitution

:p is useful with ^*old*^*new*, :s, :gs, :as, and :ags to suppress command execution. This form allows you to check the effect of substitutions. It also allows you to make several changes to a command before executing it. When you use :p with a substitution modifier, remember to include the final ^ or / delimiter, as shown below:

```
% uuencode memo.aug24 memo.aug24 > junk1    Encode the first file
% !:gs/24/25/:p                             Change input file and print command
uuencode memo.aug25 memo.aug25 > junk1
% ^1^2^:p                                   Change output file and print command
uuencode memo.aug25 memo.aug25 > junk2
% !!                                        Command is okay now; execute it
uuencode memo.aug25 memo.aug25 > junk2
```

Filename Modifiers

To extract a particular piece of a filename, you can add one of the filename modifiers onto a word designator that specifies a name. Table 6–6 demonstrates which part of the name each modifier refers to, for various filenames.

Table 6–6: Filename Modifiers

Filename	:h (head)	:t (tail)	:r (root)	:e (extension)
/usr/include/stdio.h	*/usr/include*	*stdio.h*	*/usr/include/stdio*	*h*
/usr/spool/lpd	*/usr/spool*	*lpd*	*/usr/spool/lpd*	empty
intro.ms	empty	*intro.ms*	*intro*	*ms*
README	empty	*README*	*README*	empty

Filename modifiers are useful when you need to refer to a name that's similar to one you've recently used:

```
% vi myprog.c
% make !$:r
make myprog

% diff introduction.ms.old !#^:r
diff introduction.ms.old introduction.ms

% more /usr/local/include/etm.h
% more !$:h/nio.h
more /usr/local/include/nio.h
```

You can apply filename modifiers to variable references, too. For example, to extract the tail component of your current working directory, use $cwd:t or ${cwd:t}.

Making History Persist Across Login Sessions

If you set the *savehist* shell variable, the shell saves history lines in ~/.history when you log out and rereads them the next time you log in. This feature provides history continuity across logins, so that you can reuse commands from your previous session.

If you set *savehist* without specifying a value, your entire history list is saved:

```
set history = 20
set savehist
```

If you assign *savehist* a value, it should be a number no greater than the value of the *history* shell variable:

```
set history = 20
set savehist = 10
```

If you maintain multiple logins under the same username (e.g., in a multiple window environment), the history read on each new login comes from the session from which you most recently logged out.

7

The tcsh Command-Line Editor

tcsh provides a general purpose command-line editor. You can use it to retrieve and repeat commands from your history list (either as is or in modified form), or to modify the current command. For instance, if you notice a typo at the beginning of the line, you can move the cursor to the beginning and correct the mistake, instead of erasing the command and retyping it.

The command editor is extremely useful, but it can be daunting initially. When you first try it, don't attempt to learn everything at once. Instead of trying to commit dozens of editing commands to memory in a single session, start with a few. Once you're comfortable, learn a few more. Take it slow, but stick with it—using the editor becomes increasingly natural with practice, and you'll be glad you took the time to learn it.

This chapter is organized into the following sections:

- An overview of the editing process

- How to choose a set of bindings and ensure that you get the right set at login time

- How to edit commands using the *emacs* or *vi* bindings

- How to get information about or change your current bindings

Editing a Command

You can use the editor to make arbitrarily complex changes to a command, but the editing process is conceptually quite simple. Type in a new command (or retrieve a command from your history list); if it needs modification (e.g., to create a similar command, or to fix mistakes), edit the command by adding new text or changing existing text; then hit RETURN to execute it.

To retrieve commands from your history list, navigate up and down using CTRL-P (previous command) and CTRL-N (next command).* One basic idiom you should commit to memory immediately is CTRL-P RETURN to repeat your previous command. There are also editing commands that perform searches on your history list; these commands are described later.

If you elect not to execute the command in the edit buffer, cancel it by typing your interrupt character (usually CTRL-C). Another way of "canceling" a command is to retrieve a different command into the editing buffer, e.g., with CTRL-P.

The cursor need not be at the end of the line to execute or cancel a command.

You won't have any history list from which to recall commands unless you've set the *history* shell variable. See Chapter 6, *Using Your Command History*, for instructions.

Command Key Bindings

You control the command editor interface by choosing a set of key bindings—associations between keys and editing commands. There are two sets of bindings, patterned after the editing commands used in GNU *emacs* and in *vi*.[†] If the set of bindings you want is not the set *tcsh* uses by default at your site,[‡] make sure you always get the desired bindings by adding the appropriate *bindkey* command to `~/.cshrc` or `~/.tcshrc`:

```
bindkey -e                          Select emacs bindings
bindkey -v                          Select vi bindings
```

You can also use *bindkey* commands to add, remove, or modify individual bindings. See "Examining and Modifying Key Bindings," later in this chapter.

bindkey is a *tcsh*-specific command. If you use `~/.cshrc` rather than `~/.tcshrc`, protect any *bindkey* statements from *csh*, using the instructions in the section "Organizing Your Startup Files" in Chapter 4, *The Shell Startup Files*.

Getting Key Binding Information

With either set of bindings, you'll sometimes need to review the functions of certain keys as you learn the command editor. The following command is useful:

---

* The up arrow and down arrow keys do the same thing as CTRL-P and CTRL-N.
† *tcsh* internalizes the ever-raging *emacs* vs. *vi* conflict and resolves it by accommodating users of both editors.
‡ The *emacs* bindings are usually (but not necessarily) the default. Try this command:

```
% echo $version
```

If you see the word vi in the result, *tcsh* uses the *vi* bindings by default at your site.

```
% bindkey
```

bindkey, with no arguments, displays your current key bindings by showing the associations between keystrokes and editing command names. Keystrokes are displayed using ^*X* for CTRL-*X*, ^[for ESC, ^? for DEL, and *nnn* for the ASCII character with octal code *nnn*. The *nnn* notation is obscure; typically these are keystrokes you type by holding down the META key. It's usually easier to figure out what META-*c* does by looking for the command associated with ESC *c* (displayed as ^[*c*]), because META-*c* and ESC *c* execute the same command.

If you don't know what an editing command name means, use the following command to get a list of short descriptions:

```
% bindkey -1
```

Comparison of emacs Mode and vi Mode

If you're familiar with *emacs* or *vi*, the corresponding set of command editor bindings is generally similar to what you're already used to, so you may simply want to use the bindings that most resemble whichever editor you prefer. Otherwise, you can try both sets and see which you like best. The following comparison describes some general differences between the *emacs* and *vi* bindings:

- *emacs* bindings are modeless, i.e., they are always active and you don't have to think about when you can use them. *vi* mode, by contrast, actually consists of two modes. The commands are different in each mode, and you switch between modes to do different things. The dual modes can be confusing until you get used to them.

- *emacs*, with fewer basic commands, is simpler. *vi* gives you finer control (for example, *vi* mode gives you two definitions of a word to use in word motion commands and has character-seeking motion commands).

- *emacs* mode maintains a cut buffer from which you can yank deleted text. *vi* mode does not.

- In *emacs* mode, you can set a mark. In *vi* mode, you can't.

- The command history searching capabilities differ.

emacs Editing Mode

This section describes how to edit commands using the *emacs* bindings. Be sure to select those bindings before trying any of the commands described below:

```
% bindkey -e
```

In *emacs* mode, editing commands are always active. Any character that is not an editing command is inserted into the edit buffer. Otherwise, the command is executed.

emacs Cursor Motion Commands

Before making a change (e.g., adding or deleting text), you position the cursor. The *emacs* cursor motion commands are shown in Table 7–1.

Table 7–1: Cursor Positioning Commands (emacs Mode)

Command	Description
CTRL-B	Move cursor back (left) one character
CTRL-F	Move cursor forward (right) one character
ESC b	Move cursor back one word
ESC f	Move cursor forward one word
CTRL-A	Move cursor to beginning of line
CTRL-E	Move cursor to end of line

Try these commands by entering the following line, leaving the cursor at the end:

```
% echo this is a command
```

Then, enter the editing commands below; you should see the cursor move, as shown:

```
% echo this is a command       Type CTRL-B
% echo this is a command       Type ESC b
% echo this is a command       Type CTRL-A
% echo this is a command       Type CTRL-F
% echo this is a command       Type ESC f
% echo this is a command       Type CTRL-E
```

emacs Modification Commands

To add new characters to the current command, just type them. To delete characters, words, or even the entire line, use the commands shown in Table 7–2. Modifications take place at the cursor position.

Table 7–2: Text Deletion Commands (emacs Mode)

Command	Description
DEL or CTRL-H	Delete character to left of cursor
CTRL-D	Delete character under cursor
ESC d	Delete word
ESC DEL or ESC CTRL-H	Delete word backward
CTRL-K	Delete from cursor to end of line
CTRL-U	Delete entire line

Try the modification commands by typing the following line, leaving the cursor at the end:

```
% echo My typing skilks are not amazing.█
```

Then, use the following editing commands to make the changes shown below:

```
% echo My typing skilks are not █mazing.        Type ESC b
% echo My typing skilks are █mazing.            Type ESC CTRL-H
% echo My typing skilk█ are amazing.            Type CTRL-B several times
% echo My typing skil█ are amazing.             Type CTRL-H
% echo My typing skill█ are amazing.            Type l
```

Deletion commands, other than those that clobber single characters, place the deleted text into a cut buffer. To yank the text back into the command line, use CTRL-Y. You can easily rearrange sections of the command line this way, because the text need not be returned to its original location. You can yank the text into the command line more than once. (Character deletions are not placed in the cut buffer, since you can retype a character to restore it.)

Repeating emacs Commands

If you want to repeat a command several times, it's often easier to specify a repeat count than to type the command multiple times. To repeat a command *n* times, precede it with ESC *n*, where *n* is some number. For example, ESC 10 CTRL-B moves the cursor back ten characters, and ESC 3 ESC d deletes three words. If a command cannot be repeated as many times as you specify, *tcsh* repeats it as many times as possible.

Another way to repeat a command, if it consists of a single keystroke, is simply to hold down the key.

emacs History-Searching Commands

emacs mode allows you to search your history list for a command you want to edit. This is often faster than backing up a line at a time with CTRL-P or up arrow. You can specify a command line either by a prefix of the line, or by a string that appears in the line.

To use prefix searching, enter the first part of the command line, then type ESC p. The prefix can contain filename pattern characters. *tcsh* searches backward through your history for a command that begins with the prefix and retrieves it into the edit buffer. If the command isn't the one you want, type ESC p again to find the next match. ESC n is similar but searches forward. You can use ESC p and ESC n together to bounce back and forth among the matching commands.

String searching is done using two commands that allow *emacs*-style incremental searches. These commands are not bound to any keys by default, so you must bind them to some key or key sequence before you can use them. For example, to bind them to CTRL-X p and CTRL-X n, put the following commands in your ~/.cshrc file:

```
bindkey "^xp" i-search-back
bindkey "^xn" i-search-fwd
```

These two commands allow you to search backward or forward, so that as you type a string, the command line containing that string is retrieved into the edit buffer. For example, suppose your history looks like this:

```
unexpand note.txt > note2.txt
man cal
cal 1066
```

When you type CTRL-X p, the command editor prints bck: as a prompt, and prepares to search backward for commands. If you then type a, n, and d in succession, *tcsh* retrieves commands into the edit buffer in the following order:

```
cal 1066                          Command matches a
man cal                           Command matches an
unexpand note.txt > note2.txt     Command matches and
```

With incremental searching, you type no more than necessary to find the desired command, and the text you type can be anywhere in the command line. If you enter an extra character, delete it and the search will return to the previous command found.

Hit ESC to terminate an incremental search, so that you can edit the currently displayed command. Or, just hit RETURN to execute the command.

Using the Arrow Keys in emacs Mode

You can use the arrow keys for *emacs* mode editing. Up arrow and down arrow move up and down through your history list, like CTRL-P and CTRL-N. Left arrow and right arrow move the cursor left and right one character, like CTRL-B and CTRL-F.

vi Editing Mode

This section describes how to edit commands using the *vi* bindings. Be sure to select those bindings before trying any of the commands described below:

```
% bindkey -v
```

The *vi* bindings provide capabilities similar to those of the *emacs* bindings, but they have their own distinctive characteristics. The keystrokes to perform the commands sometimes differ, of course; a more significant difference is that editing using the *vi* bindings really involves two modes—just as with *vi* itself. In *vi* insert mode, characters are placed in the edit buffer as you type them. In *vi* command mode, characters are interpreted as editing commands. For example, if you type an x in insert mode, an x is put into the command line at the cursor position. If you type an x in command mode, the character under the cursor is deleted.

Because the two *vi* modes behave differently, it's important to know the rules for switching between them:

- The editor is in insert mode initially, e.g., if you're typing a new command, or if you've just retrieved a line from your history list into the edit buffer, using CTRL-P.

- To enter command mode, hit ESC.

- In command mode, several commands put you into insert mode for entering new text, e.g., a (append after cursor) or i (insert before cursor). From insert mode, you can return to command mode by hitting ESC.

- If you're not sure what mode you're in, hit ESC until *tcsh* beeps. You will then be in *vi* command mode.

The dual modes may seem confusing, but they're such an integral part of *vi* editing mode that they quickly become second nature. Some of the most common editing commands work in either mode, which helps alleviate confusion. For example, CTRL-P and CTRL-N move up and down through the history list, and RETURN and CTRL-C execute and cancel the current command, no matter which mode you're in.

Using vi Insert Mode

When you begin to edit a command using the *vi* bindings, you're in insert mode and most characters simply go into the edit buffer at the cursor position. You can do some limited cursor movement and text deletion using the commands listed in Table 7-3.

Table 7-3: Editing Commands Available in vi Insert Mode

Command	Description
CTRL-B	Move cursor back (left) one character
CTRL-F	Move cursor forward (right) one character
CTRL-A	Move cursor to beginning of line
CTRL-E	Move cursor to end of line
DEL or CTRL-H	Delete character to left of cursor
CTRL-W	Delete word backward
CTRL-U	Delete from beginning of line to cursor
CTRL-K	Delete from cursor to end of line

Using vi Command Mode

To make changes that cannot easily be made in insert mode, hit ESC to enter command mode. The commands for moving the cursor, changing text, or deleting text in command mode are more flexible than those available in insert mode. (There is also a u command that is supposed to undo the last change made in command mode; unfortunately, I have not found it to work reliably.)

Cursor motion commands

Table 7–4 lists some of the cursor motion commands that you can use in command mode. The word motion commands w, b, and e stop at whitespace or punctuation, whereas W, B, and E stop only at whitespace. Consequently, you can produce larger cursor motions with the uppercase commands, whereas the lowercase commands are useful for finer motions such as bouncing along successive components of pathnames.

0 is similar to ^ and CTRL-A, but 0 moves to the first column of the command, whereas ^ and CTRL-A move to the first non-whitespace character.

Table 7–4: Cursor Positioning Commands (vi Command Mode)

Command	Description
h or CTRL-H	Move cursor back (left) one character
l or SPACE	Move cursor forward (right) one character
w	Move cursor forward (right) one word
b	Move cursor back (left) one word
e	Move cursor to next word ending
W, B, E	Like w, b, and e, but different word definition
^ or CTRL-A	Move cursor to beginning of line (first non-whitespace character)
0	Move cursor to beginning of line
$ or CTRL-E	Move cursor to end of line

Try the *vi* command mode motion commands by entering the following line, leaving the cursor at the end of the line:

```
% echo this is a command
```

Hit ESC to enter command mode, then type the following commands. You should see the cursor move as shown below:

```
% echo this is a command          Type h
% echo this is a command          Type b
% echo this is a command          Type ^ or CTRL-A
% echo this is a command          Type SPACE or l
% echo this is a command          Type w
% echo this is a command          Type $ or CTRL-E
```

Repeating commands

Motion commands can be repeated in *vi* command mode by preceding the command with a number. For instance, 3b moves backward three words and 15 SPACE moves forward 15 characters. 0 is not a valid repeat count because 0 is itself a command (move the cursor to the start of the line).

Many of the *vi* command mode modification commands, described below, can take a repeat count. The command descriptions indicate which can and which can't.

Adding text

To add text when you're in command mode, use one of the commands in Table 7–5 to enter insert mode, then start typing. New text is added to the command buffer until you hit ESC to return to command mode.

Repeat counts do not work for the commands listed in Table 7–5.

Table 7–5: Text Insertion Commands (vi Command Mode)

Command	Description
a	Append new text after cursor until ESC
i	Insert new text before cursor until ESC
A	Append new text after end of line until ESC
I	Insert new text before beginning of line until ESC

Deleting text

The commands shown in Table 7–6 delete text from the edit buffer. x and X delete single characters. The d*m* command is useful for deleting units of text—it deletes from the cursor to wherever the motion command *m* would place the cursor. For instance, dw and db delete a word forward or backward.

Command mode deletion commands can take repeat counts, e.g., 3dw (or d3w) deletes three words and 5x deletes five characters.

Table 7–6: Text Deletion Commands (vi Command Mode)

Command	Description
x	Delete character under cursor
X or DEL	Delete character to left of cursor
d*m*	Delete from cursor to end of motion command *m*
D	Synonym for d$
CTRL-W	Delete word backward

Table 7–6: Text Deletion Commands (vi Command Mode) (continued)

Command	Description
CTRL-U	Delete from beginning of line to cursor
CTRL-K	Delete from cursor to end of line

Replacing text

To replace part of the edit buffer, you can delete the old text, then insert the new text. However, *vi* command mode offers a set of text replacement commands that combine the delete and insert operations (see Table 7–7). The c*m* command acts like d*m*, but also puts you in insert mode. For instance, to change a word, type cw, then type the new word and hit ESC. To replace the character under the cursor, type r, then the new character. R puts you in replace mode, which replaces characters as you type, until you hit ESC. The s command substitutes characters that you type for the character under the cursor, until you hit ESC.

The c and s commands can be given a repeat count. For instance, 4cw (or c4w) changes four words, and 6s substitutes six characters beginning with the one under the cursor, using the text you type following the command.

Table 7–7: Text Replacement Commands (vi Command Mode)

Command	Description
c*m*	Change characters from cursor to end of motion command *m* until ESC
C	Synonym for c$
r*c*	Replace character under cursor with character *c*
R	Replace multiple characters until ESC
s	Substitute character under cursor with characters typed until ESC

To see how *vi* command mode editing works, try the following:

```
% echo My typing skilks are not amazing.█   Type a simple command line
% echo My typing skilks are not █mazing.    Hit ESC to enter command mode, then type b
% echo My typing skilks are █mazing.        Type db
% echo My typing skil█s are amazing.        Type h several times
% echo My typing skil█s are amazing.        Type rl
```

vi History-Searching Commands

In *vi* command mode, you can use ? and / to search backward and forward through your history list. For instance, when you type ?, *tcsh* prints ? as a prompt to solicit the string you want to search for. Type a string and hit RETURN. The string can contain filename pattern characters. The editor searches backward for a line that matches the string and retrieves it into the edit buffer, with the cursor at the end of the line. If the command isn't the one you want, type n (next match) to repeat the search in the same direction. N repeats the search in the opposite direction. You can use n and N together to bounce back and forth among the matching commands.

When you find the command you want, just start editing it as usual (note that you'll still be in command mode after a search). Or, you can hit RETURN to execute it.

vi Character-Seeking Commands

vi command mode provides a set of commands that search for characters in the current command line (see Table 7–8). You can use these as motion commands to move the cursor to a particular character, or combine them with the d or c commands to delete or change text from the cursor position to that character.

Table 7–8: Character-Seeking Motion Commands (vi Command Mode)

Command	Description
fc	Move cursor to next instance of *c* in line
Fc	Move cursor to previous instance of *c* in line
tc	Move cursor up to next instance of *c* in line
Tc	Move cursor back to previous instance of *c* in line
;	Repeat previous f or F command
,	Repeat previous f or F command in opposite direction

f*c* moves the cursor forward to the next instance of character *c* in the command. F*c* moves the cursor backward:

```
% echo abcdefghi█       Type a command, leaving cursor at end
% echo abcdefghi        Type ESC to enter command mode, then Fo to move back to o
% echo abcdefghi        Type fg to move forward to g
```

The ; command repeats the last f or F command. The , command is similar but moves the cursor in the opposite direction. That is, the , command repeats f as F and F as f. This feature is useful if you use multiple ; commands to search for successive instances of a character, and go too far:

```
% echo three games of tic tac toe█     Type a command, leaving cursor at end
% echo three games of tic tac toe      Hit ESC to enter command mode, then type Ft
% echo three games of tic tac toe      Type ; to repeat search
% echo three games of tic tac toe      Type ; to repeat search
% echo three games of tic tac toe      Type ; to repeat search
% echo three games of tic tac toe      Oops, too far; type , to reverse search
```

tc and Tc are similar to fc and Fc, but the former move the cursor up to or back to the *c*, i.e., just to the left of *c* for t and just to the right of *c* for T.

You can precede the character-seeking commands with d or c to delete or change text. For example, dt/ deletes up to the next slash (handy for clobbering parts of pathnames) and 3c SPACE changes text up through the third space after the cursor.

Using the Arrow Keys in vi Mode

Up arrow and down arrow are like CTRL-P and CTRL-N, just as in *emacs* mode. Left arrow and right arrow move the cursor left and right one character. However, there is a quirk you should look out for if you're in insert mode. On many terminals, arrow keys actually send out strings of characters that begin with ESC. Although the arrow keys move the cursor, they'll also switch you into command mode. If you find this distracting, avoid left arrow and right arrow in insert mode, and stick with CTRL-B and CTRL-F.

Examining and Modifying Key Bindings

tcsh lets you display and change your key bindings using the *bindkey* command. The various forms of *bindkey* are summarized in Table 7–9, and discussed below.

Table 7–9: Forms of the bindkey Command

Command	Description
bindkey -e	Select *emacs* bindings
bindkey -v	Select *vi* bindings
bindkey -d	Restore default bindings
bindkey -u	Display *bindkey* usage message
bindkey -l	List editing commands and their meanings
bindkey	List all key bindings
bindkey *key*	List binding for *key*
bindkey *key cmd*	Bind *key* to editing command *cmd*
bindkey -c *key cmd*	Bind *key* to UNIX command *cmd*
bindkey -s *key str*	Bind *key* to string *str*
bindkey -r *key*	Remove binding for *key*

The forms of *bindkey* that take a *key* argument also allow the following flags:

–k Allows *key* to be up, down, left, or right, to indicate an arrow key.

–b Allows *key* to be C-*X* or M-*X*, to indicate CTRL-*X* or META-*X*.

–a Allows you to specify the alternate key map (the map used for *vi* command mode).

-- May be used immediately preceding *key* to tell *bindkey* to stop processing arguments as flags. This flag is useful when *key* itself begins with a dash.

–k and *–b* cannot both be used in the same command.

Selecting a Set of Bindings

To select a set of bindings en masse, use the *–e* or *–v* option:

```
% bindkey -e          Select emacs bindings
% bindkey -v          Select vi bindings
```

Selecting either set rebinds every key to the default for that set, undoing any prior bindings you may have established. To bind any individual keys specially (as discussed under "Changing Key Bindings," below), you should do so only after executing *bindkey –e* or *bindkey –v*.

bindkey –d restores all bindings to whatever the default set is at your site. This isn't really useful, unless you're using whatever set that happens to be. You might as well use *bindkey –e* or *bindkey –v* to explicitly select a particular set.

Getting a List of Editing Commands

To see the full list of editing command names and their meanings, use the following command:

```
% bindkey -l
backward-char
      Move back a character
backward-delete-char
      Delete the character behind cursor
backward-delete-word
      Cut from beginning of current word to cursor - saved in cut buffer
      ⋮
```

bindkey –l is useful for determining which editing commands can be bound to keys, or what a given command does. The descriptions displayed are quite concise, however. Appendix C, *Other Sources of Information*, lists a document that provides more detailed explanations of the editing commands.

Displaying Key Bindings

bindkey can display all key bindings currently in effect, or the bindings for individual keys.

Displaying all bindings

bindkey, with no arguments, lists all current key bindings:

```
% bindkey
Standard key bindings
"^@"            ->  set-mark-command
"^A"            ->  beginning-of-line
"^B"            ->  backward-char
"^C"            ->  tty-sigintr
"^D"            ->  delete-char-or-list-or-eof
    :
    :
```

To make the output more manageable, use *grep*. For example, to find out which keys are bound to commands that access the history list, type the following command:

```
% bindkey | grep history
```

bindkey reports keystrokes using the notation shown in Table 7–10. Characters that have bit 8 turned on (usually typed using the META key, if you have one) are reported using *nnn* notation.

Table 7–10: bindkey Keystroke Notation

Sequence	Character Represented by Sequence
^*X*	CTRL–*X*
^[	ESC
^?	DEL
nnn	ASCII character with octal code *nnn*

The key binding list displayed by *bindkey* is divided into four sections:

Standard key bindings
Commands bound to single keystrokes in the standard key map. For the *vi* bindings, these are the commands that are active while you are in insert mode.

Alternative key bindings
Bindings for the alternative key map. These are single-character bindings that are active during *vi* command mode. This section is empty if you use *emacs* bindings because there is no "command mode," and thus no alternative key map.

Multicharacter key bindings
Commands bound to multiple-keystroke sequences.

Arrow key bindings
Commands bound to the arrow keys.

Displaying individual key bindings

To display a single binding, name the key or key sequence in which you're interested:

```
% bindkey ^A                          Show binding for CTRL-A
"^A"    ->    beginning-of-line
% bindkey ^L                          Show binding for CTRL-L
"^L"    ->    clear-screen
```

If you name a single character *key* argument, *bindkey* displays the binding from the standard key map. For the *vi* bindings, this display corresponds to the key's meaning in insert mode. To see what the key means in *vi* command mode, use the *-a* option to display the binding from the alternative key map:

```
% bindkey !                           Show binding from standard key map
"!"    ->    self-insert-char
% bindkey -a !                        Show binding from alternative key map
"!"    ->    expand-history
```

Specifying the key Argument

The *key* argument to *bindkey* can represent a single character or a string of characters. *key* can include special characters, and some of *bindkey*'s options modify the *key* argument's interpretation.

The following methods allow you to include special characters in *key*:

- Use caret notation to denote control characters, e.g., ^A or ^a for CTRL-A. Also, ^[means ESC, and ^? means DEL.

- Precede a special character with CTRL-V to turn off its special meaning.

- Put *key* in quotes.

- Use one of the backslash sequences shown in Table 7-11. Putting a backslash in front of a character that's not listed in the table turns off any special meaning the character might have.

Table 7-11: bindkey Special Character Sequences

Sequence	Character Represented by Sequence
^X	CTRL-X
^[	ESC
^?	DEL
\^	^
\a	CTRL-G (bell)
\b	CTRL-H
\e	ESC
\f	FORMFEED

Table 7-11: bindkey Special Character Sequences (continued)

Sequence	Character Represented by Sequence
\n	NEWLINE
\r	RETURN
\t	TAB
\v	CTRL-K (vertical tab)
\nnn	ASCII character with octal code nnn

For example, to check the binding for CTRL-C, you can type any of these commands:

```
% bindkey ^C
% bindkey CTRL-V CTRL-C
% bindkey "\003"
% bindkey \\003
```

In general, it's a good idea to put quotes around a *key* argument that contains backslash sequences or characters that the shell interprets specially, like | or ; or (. Note that you type a backslash only once if it's used within quotes, but twice if it's not in quotes.

Options that modify interpretation of the key argument

To specify an arrow key, use the $-k$ option and left, right, up, or down as the key name, e.g.:

```
% bindkey -k left              Display binding for left arrow key
```

The $-b$ option allows you to use C-*X* or M-*X* notation to specify control or META characters:

```
% bindkey -b C-A               Show binding for CTRL-A
% bindkey -b M-A               Show binding for META-A
```

If you use an arrow key name or C-*X*/M-*X* but forget the $-k$ or $-b$ option, the *key* argument is interpreted as a multicharacter sequence, which won't give you the results you're looking for:

```
% bindkey left
Unbound extended key "left"
% bindkey C-A
Unbound extended key "C-A"
```

The *tcsh* manual page says that $-b$ allows F-*n* notation to be used for specifying function keys. Unfortunately, this feature doesn't work.

Changing Key Bindings

You can customize your bindings by modifying bindings for individual keys. *bind-key* allows you to do the following:

- Assign a new binding

- Remove a binding

- Bind a key to a UNIX command

- Bind a key to a literal string

You can experiment with your bindings by changing them at the command line, using the *bindkey* commands described below. If you decide to make a given binding part of your environment, put the appropriate command in `~/.cshrc`.

Binding an individual key

To associate an editing command with a key, bind the command to the key:

```
% bindkey key command
```

key is indicated as described previously, under "Specifying the key Argument." *command* is any of the editing command names listed by *bindkey −l*.

If you edit in *vi* mode, individual key bindings are installed by default in the standard key map, which applies to *vi* insert mode. To establish a binding for use in *vi* command mode, use the *−a* option to install the binding in the alternative key map. For instance, CTRL-B and CTRL-F are normally unbound in *vi* command mode. To give these keys the same meaning in command mode that they have in insert mode, use the following commands:

```
% bindkey -a ^B backward-char
% bindkey -a ^F forward-char
```

−a can be used with *−b* or *−k*, or with the *−c*, *−d*, *−r*, and *−s* options, described below.

Binding a key to itself

To bind a key to itself, bind it to *self-insert-command*:

```
% bindkey key self-insert-command
```

In effect, this binding turns off any special meaning the key has for editing, so that when you type the key it appears as itself in the command line. Most alphanumeric keys are bound to *self-insert-command* in *emacs* mode and *vi* insert mode.

Removing a binding

To unbind a key, remove the binding:

```
% bindkey -r key
```

Removing a binding is different than binding the key to itself. A self-bound key appears as itself in the command line when you type it, whereas a key that's been unbound becomes dead, i.e., when you type it, nothing happens.

Binding a key to a shell command

bindkey −c lets you bind a key to UNIX commands. For example, if you'd like CTRL-X 1 to run *ls −l |more*, use the following binding:

```
% bindkey -c ^X1 'ls -l|more'
```

When you type a key or key sequence that's bound to a UNIX command, the current command line remains intact. That is, the UNIX command is executed immediately, and when it has finished, the command line is redisplayed as it was before you typed the key sequence.

It's not necessary to include a newline at the end of the command string. You can include special characters in the command, just as you can include special characters in *key*, as described above in "Specifying the key Argument." However, caret sequences inside quotes are interpreted literally in this usage.

Binding a key to a literal string

bindkey −s lets you bind a key to a literal string:

```
% bindkey -s key string
```

Typing *key* becomes equivalent to typing *string*. You can include special characters in *string* as you do in *key* (see "Specifying the key Argument"), except that caret sequences inside quotes are interpreted literally.

If *string* contains other editing commands, they are interpreted as such when you use *key* in a command line.

Binding a key to a string can be used to assign pieces of UNIX commands to keys. Suppose you often search for processes using this command:

```
% ps ax | grep string
```

You could assign the first part of the command to a key sequence, e.g., CTRL-X p:

```
% bindkey -s ^Xp 'ps ax | grep '
```

Then, to search for, say, *emacs* processes, you could type the following:

```
% CTRL-X pemacs
```

Conflicts Between Terminal Settings and Key Bindings

If a key doesn't do what you expect, you may have a conflict between the way the terminal driver and the command editor are interpreting keystrokes. For example, CTRL-W is normally interpreted as the **werase** (word erase) character by the terminal driver. But CTRL-W doesn't perform the word erase function if you use the *emacs* bindings, because CTRL-W is bound to the editor's *kill-region* command. If you suspect a conflict, you can change the terminal driver setting using *stty* (see Chapter 5, *Setting Up Your Terminal*), or change the command editor key binding using *bindkey*.

Conflicts Between Key Bindings

If you specify two multicharacter bindings that begin with the same prefix, you will not be able to use both bindings. Instead, the second binding replaces the first:

```
% bindkey -s ^Xl ls
% bindkey -s ^Xlm 'ls | more'
```

8

Using Aliases To Create Command Shortcuts

As you use the shell, you'll notice patterns in the way you work. Once you do, you can save typing by using the shell's aliasing mechanism to create short alternate names for frequently used commands or command sequences. This chapter discusses how to define and remove aliases, ways in which aliases are useful, and how to manage multiple sets of aliases.

Defining Aliases

An alias definition has the following form:

```
alias name definition
```

name is what you want to call the alias, and *definition* is the command to run when you use *name* as a command. For example, the following aliases allow you to use *h* and *m* as short names for the *history* and *more* commands:

```
alias h history
alias m more
```

Aliases are best placed in your ˜/.cshrc file so that they're available to your login shell as well as any subshells. However, don't put an alias in ˜/.cshrc until you've verified that it works correctly. First, define the alias at the command line, and then test it:

```
% alias h history          Define the alias
% h                        Try it out
```

If an alias doesn't work as you expect, use one of the following commands to determine how the shell is interpreting your definition:

```
% alias name                    Show definition for alias name
% alias                         Show definitions for all aliases
```

To get rid of an alias, use *unalias*:

```
% unalias name                  Remove alias name
% unalias *                     Remove all aliases
```

unalias is especially useful when you're testing an alias at the command line, and then decide you don't want it to use it, after all. *unalias* can also be used in `~/.cshrc` to undo the effects of a system-wide startup file like `/etc/csh.cshrc`. Such a file might be processed automatically before your own startup files, and could contain system aliases that you don't want. Use *unalias* to remove them.

Aliases are used in the same manner as commands. They can take arguments:

```
% h 5                           Review the last five commands in your history list
% m ~/.cshrc                    Look at your ~/.cshrc file
```

They can be used in pipes:

```
% grep -i fang *.ms | m         Search for a string, using more to page the output
```

Alias definitions can contain spaces:

```
alias .. cd ..                  Make .. an alias for cd ..
```

But, you must quote definitions that contain special characters like **;** or **|** or *****:

```
alias nusers 'who | wc -l'      Create alias to count the number of users
```

Aliases can refer to other aliases:

```
alias hm 'h | m'                Make hm equivalent to history | more
```

Be careful to avoid alias loops:

```
alias x y
alias y x
```

The shell detects the loop and warns you about it:

```
% x
Alias loop.
% y
Alias loop.
```

An alias is special only when used as a command name:

```
% h                 h expands to history here
% echo h            Here, h is just h
```

Referring to Arguments in Aliases

By default, arguments that follow an alias are the same as arguments following the command the alias signifies. Consider the following alias, which defines a command *ll* to generate a long directory listing:

```
alias ll ls -l
```

Any arguments to *ll* are added to the end of the *ls* command:

% ll	Becomes *ls –l*
% ll -R	Becomes *ls –l –R*
% ll /bin /etc	Becomes *ls –l /bin /etc*

If you want the arguments to be located somewhere other than the end of the command, use \!* to indicate where. When you invoke the alias, \!* expands to the arguments you specify, or to nothing if there are no arguments. The following alias defines a command *llm* that generates a long listing, and runs it through *more*:

```
alias llm 'ls -l \!* | more'
```

The definition uses \!* to make sure that any arguments are associated with *ls*, and not with *more*:

% llm	Becomes *ls –l	more*
% llm -R	Becomes *ls –l –R	more*
% llm /bin /etc	Becomes *ls –l /bin /etc	more*

You can also use \!^ and \!$ to refer to the first and last arguments.

Use \!:*n* to refer to specific arguments by position, such as \!:2 for the second argument or \!:0 for the command name. For example, if you keep mail files in a directory named *~/Mail*, you can create aliases that let you easily copy files in and out of that directory:

```
alias tobox 'cp \!:1 ~/Mail/\!:2'
alias frombox 'cp ~/Mail/\!:1 \!:2'
```

Arguments referred to using \!^ or \!:*n* must be supplied when the alias is invoked, or an error occurs:

% frombox mesg1	Argument two missing
Bad ! arg selector.	

Referring to the History List in Aliases

It's not common to refer to your history list in an alias, but you can do it, and the feature can be quite useful. The previous command is the one you'll probably want to use most. Since !! refers to your previous command at the command line, you might expect \!\! to do so in an alias. Unfortunately, you'd be wrong. You have to use \!-1 instead. Thus, to create an alias for looking at the file named by the final argument of your previous command, use \!-1$, as shown below:

```
alias mf 'more \!-1$'
```

Getting Used to Aliases

After you define an alias, remember to use it. "Why, that's completely obvious," you say. Actually, it's not. You may be so used to typing the long form of commands that you have a mental habit you need to break. Once you learn to use aliases consistently, you'll realize a gain in keyboard efficiency.

Run *alias* from time to time, without arguments, to review your aliases. That way, you can see if you've forgotten any aliases that you should be using. You might even discover some that haven't proven worthwhile, and can be deleted from your *~/.cshrc* file.

Uses for Aliases

This section describes various ways you can put aliases to work, making it easier to issue commands.

Aliases Save Typing

One of the principal benefits of aliases is that they save typing. They can achieve this end in many different ways, as shown below:

- To provide shorter names for commands:

  ```
  alias m more                    Map m to more
  alias j jobs                    Map j to jobs
  ```

- To string commands together in a pipeline:

  ```
  alias wsm 'who | sort | more'   Define wsm as sorted, paged who command
  alias print 'pr \!* | lpr'      Print files
  ```

- To execute a sequence of commands:

  ```
  alias cl 'cd \!* ; ls'          Change to directory, then list it
  ```

- To construct commands that supply default arguments to other commands:

  ```
  alias askrm rm -i               Define safer rm command
  alias gora gopher gopher.ora.com   Connect to gopher.ora.com
  ```

- To move into commonly used directories:

  ```
  alias .. cd ..                  Move to parent directory
  alias mq cd /usr/spool/mqueue   Move to mail queue directory
  ```

Aliases Can Redefine Commands

An alias name can be the same as the command invoked by the alias definition. This is a special case that's not a loop. Instead, it effectively changes the normal meaning of the command. For instance, if you usually do case-insensitive searches when you use *grep*, you can alias *grep* to supply the *-i* argument by default:

```
alias grep grep -i
```

To use the command name with its original meaning, precede it with a backslash, or invoke the command using its full pathname:

```
% \grep hognose *.ms
% /bin/grep hognose *.ms
```

It's not a good idea to redefine the meaning of dangerous commands, however. For example, you might try the following alias as a way of making *rm* safer:

```
alias rm rm -i
```

The effect of using this alias is that you start expecting *rm* to prompt you by default. This assumption can lead to disaster.[*] It's better to use a different alias name for safe removals, and leave *rm* alone:

```
alias askrm rm -i
```

Aliases Hide Differences Between Systems

If you have accounts on several types of UNIX machines, you've no doubt found differences in the commands provided on each. Aliases can provide a more consistent working environment by masking differences between systems. By putting a little thought into appropriate aliases, you can avoid eventual problems with differences in commands. Follow the guidelines below:

- At my site, the command to send a file to a printer depends on whether a machine is running the BSD or System V print spooler. For instance, to print on *lwa*, I'd use one of the following commands:

`% lpr -Plwa file`	BSD version
`% lp -dlwa file`	System V version

  Because I don't want to remember these differences, I can create an alias (*lwa*) to do the "right" thing on each system:

`alias lwa lpr -Plwa`	BSD version
`alias lwa lp -dlwa`	System V version

---

[*] Suppose you move to another account where the same alias isn't in effect. Or, suppose a friend comes to you and asks how to remove a bunch of files and you say, "Just use *rm* *. It'll ask you to confirm each removal." In fact, it won't, unless your soon-to-be-former friend has the same alias.

By putting the appropriate alias in each of my *˜/.cshrc* files, I can use the same command on any machine to send a file to *lwa*:

```
% lwa psfile
```

- One of my UNIX machines provides a command, *ll*, that acts like *ls −l*. The others don't, but I can use an alias on those to achieve the same effect:

```
alias ll ls -l
```

Now, I can use *ll* no matter where I'm logged in.

- I frequently need to determine whether certain programs are running, using *ps* to generate the process list and *grep* to search through it. The *ps* options for listing all processes are different for BSD and System V versions of UNIX. Fortunately, the difference can be hidden inside aliases that use the options appropriate to each kind of system:

```
alias psg 'ps ax | grep'          BSD version
alias psg 'ps -ef | grep'         System V version
```

Consequently, I can search for processes the same way from any of my accounts:

```
% psg sendmail                     See how many sendmail processes there are
% psg q5                           List processes on ttyq5
```

- Aliases can make *csh* look more like *tcsh*, if you don't have *tcsh*. For example, in *tcsh* CTRL-L clears the screen, which is easier than typing the *clear* command. In *csh*, you can simulate the same function, by using an alias for CTRL-L (you might have to type CTRL-V before the CTRL-L for the editor to accept the command):

```
alias  CTRL-L  clear
```

Using this alias in *csh* is slightly different from typing CTRL-L in *tcsh*, since you need to type RETURN after it. It nonetheless reduces the command name from five characters to one.

Using Sets of Aliases

The more alias definitions your *˜/.cshrc* file contains, the longer it takes the shell to start up. On fast machines, the delay won't be much of an issue; however, on slow machines, you may find the delay frustrating. Logins and subshells (started as shell escapes from an editor or mailer, for instance) may take noticeably longer.

If some of your aliases are used only under special circumstances, consider taking them out of *˜/.cshrc* to make startup time shorter. For example, if you have aliases that are used only for a particular project, put them in a file called *proj-aliases* and locate it in the project's top-level directory. Then, when you move into that directory to work on the project, activate the aliases, as follows:

```
% cd ~/myproj
% source proj-aliases
```

(The *source* command is needed only once per login session.) If you want to be trickier, you can create an alias in *~/.cshrc* that changes into the project directory and automatically reads in the alias definitions:

```
alias cdproj 'cd ~/myproj;source proj-aliases'
```

In This Chapter:
- *Using Filename*
  Patterns
- *Using {} To Generate*
  Arguments
- *Directory Naming*
  Shorthand

9

File-Naming Shortcuts

Many commands accept multiple filenames on the command line, but typing ten or 20 names—even one or two, if they're long—can quickly become tedious. This chapter discusses several shortcuts that the shell provides for specifying filenames, so you can enter commands with less typing:

- Pattern operators, for matching filenames

- { }, for generating arguments using specific strings

- ˜*name* and =*n*, for referring to home directories and directory stack entries

Using Filename Patterns

The shell lets you specify filenames using a pattern, which is a notation that matches a group of filenames. Patterns are convenient because you can use them as a form of typing shorthand, and let the shell do the work of figuring out which filenames apply. You don't have to type them yourself. The pattern-matching characters are shown in Table 9–1.

Table 9–1: Filename-Matching Pattern Operators

Operator	Description
*	Match an arbitrary length sequence of characters
?	Match a single character
[...]	Match any character named between brackets
[^...]	Match any character not named between brackets (*tcsh* only)
^*pattern*	Match filenames not matching *pattern* (*tcsh* only)

In order to see how various patterns work, it's helpful to have some sample file-names to work with. Assume you're in a directory containing the following files:

```
% ls
Imakefile      makefile       part3      part8      xprog.h
Makefile       oot-greet.tar  part4      part9      xprog.o
Makefile.bak   part1          part5      xprog
argyle.tar     part10         part6      xprog.c
blrgle.tar.gz  part2          part7      xprog.c.bak
```

Matching Multiple Characters

The asterisk (*) acts as a wildcard, matching any string. Thus, an asterisk by itself gives you a simple way of selecting all the files in a directory. To limit the match, combine * with a partial filename:

```
% ls part*
part1      part2      part4      part6      part8
part10     part3      part5      part7      part9
% ls part1*
part1      part10
% ls *tar
argyle.tar     oot-greet.tar
% ls *tar*
argyle.tar     blrgle.tar.gz  oot-greet.tar
% ls M*e
Makefile
```

There are two subtle points about * that you should be aware of:

- * can match zero characters, not just one or more. For example, part1* matches *part10* because the * matches the final 0. The pattern also matches *part1* because the * matches the null string.

- The meaning of * is slightly different in the shell than it is in *grep, sed,* and editors like *ex* and *vi*. In the shell, part* means, "part, followed by any-thing." In *grep, sed,* and the editors, the effect of * depends on the preceding character, so part* means "par, followed by any number of t's."

Although * is most commonly used in patterns to match multiple names, you can use a wildcard pattern as a short way of typing a single name. For example, if *blrgle.tar.gz* is the only file in your current directory that begins with *bl* or ends with *.gz*, the following three commands are equivalent, but the last two are easier to type:

```
% gunzip blrgle.tar.gz
% gunzip bl*
% gunzip *.gz
```

Matching Single Characters

The question mark (?) matches any single character:

```
% ls part?
part1          part3          part5          part7          part9
part2          part4          part6          part8
% ls part??
part10
% ls xprog.?
xprog.c        xprog.h        xprog.o
% ls ?akefile
Makefile       makefile
```

The bracket notation ([...]) specifies a character class. It matches any single character named between the brackets:

```
% ls part[1248]
part1          part2          part4          part8
% ls xprog.[ch]
xprog.c        xprog.h
% ls [mM]akefile
Makefile       makefile
```

To name a range of characters, use a dash:

```
% ls part[3-7]
part3          part4          part5          part6          part7
```

To indicate a literal dash as one of the characters in the class, make it the first of the characters named between the brackets. For instance, the class [-.] matches a dash or a dot. (*tcsh* and some versions of *csh* allow the dash to be at the beginning or the end of the class, so that [-.] and [.-] are equivalent.)

Combining Pattern Operators

Multiple pattern operators can be used in a single pattern. The first pattern below matches filenames at least ten characters long, the second matches filenames containing a period or uppercase letter:

```
% ls ??????????*
Makefile.bak   argyle.tar     blrgle.tar.gz  oot-greet.tar  xprog.c.bak
% ls *[.A-Z]*
Imakefile      Makefile.bak   blrgle.tar.gz  xprog.c        xprog.h
Makefile       argyle.tar     oot-greet.tar  xprog.c.bak    xprog.o
```

Patterns and Dot Files

Our example directory actually contains dot files (files with names that begin with a period). Dot files are "invisible" in the sense that *ls* doesn't list them unless you specify the *−a* ("show all") option:

```
% ls -a
.                 Makefile.bak    part1      part5      xprog
..                argyle.tar      part10     part6      xprog.c
.exrc             blrgle.tar.gz   part2      part7      xprog.c.bak
Imakefile         makefile        part3      part8      xprog.h
Makefile          oot-greet.tar   part4      part9      xprog.o
```

Pattern matching treats dot files specially, too: filenames with a leading dot are not normally considered match candidates. A pattern must explicitly begin with a period to match them:

```
% echo *cshrc ?cshrc [.]cshrc        These patterns do not match .cshrc
echo: No match.
% echo .c* .c????                    These patterns do match .cshrc
.cshrc .cshrc
```

Negating Patterns

In *tcsh*, ^ negates a pattern match in two contexts. First, `^pattern` matches any filename that doesn't match `pattern`:

```
% ls x*
xprog          xprog.c          xprog.c.bak      xprog.h          xprog.o
% ls ^x*
Imakefile      blrgle.tar.gz    part10           part5            part9
Makefile       makefile         part2            part6
Makefile.bak   oot-greet.tar    part3            part7
argyle.tar     part1            part4            part8
```

Second, [^...] matches any single character that isn't named between the brackets:

```
% ls part[1-4]
part1          part2            part3            part4
% ls part[^1-4]
part5          part6            part7            part8            part9
% ls [mM]*file
Makefile       makefile
% ls [^mM]*file
Imakefile
```

`^pattern` isn't treated specially unless `pattern` really is a pattern, rather then a literal string. That is, `pattern` must contain at least one of the wildcard characters: *, ?, or [...]. However, if you want to match all filenames except one, you can often add * to the name to make it a pattern (e.g., `^xyz*` will match everything but xyz). This method works as long as the name isn't a prefix of another filename.

Be Careful with Patterns

Patterns can get you into trouble if you're not careful. For example, you could get into trouble if you intend to type something like the first command below, but type the second instead:

```
% rm abc*
% rm abc *
```

The second command removes *abc* along with all files matching *; that is, it removes all the files in your current directory. With some advance preparation, you can guard against this kind of disaster. If you're using *tcsh*, set the *rmstar* variable in your `~/.cshrc` file to avoid bulk removal of your files, as shown below:

```
set rmstar
```

When *rmstar* is set, *tcsh* asks whether or not you really mean it if you issue an *rm* command with * as one of the arguments. That gives you a chance to back out:

```
% rm abc *
Do you really want to delete all files? [n/y] n
```

The *rmstar* mechanism works even if *rm* is referenced from within an alias. If you're sure you want to override it, use *rm −f* ("force removal").

If you're using *csh* (which doesn't recognize *rmstar*), or if you just want to create a command that doesn't go ahead and blithely remove files, create a file-removal alias that always asks for confirmation:

```
alias askrm rm -i
```

Then, develop a habit of using *askrm* as your standard file removal command. The *−i* option causes *rm* to operate interactively: for each file to be deleted, it prompts you for confirmation. At those times when you don't want to be prompted, use *rm* instead of *askrm*.

Sometimes, people alias *rm* to *rm −i*. Chapter 8, *Using Aliases To Create Command Shortcuts*, discusses why you shouldn't do this.

Pretesting Filename Patterns

Patterns are powerful, but you may not always be sure what filenames match a given pattern, especially when you're first learning to use patterns, or when a directory contains a lot of files. *echo* is a good tool for pretesting patterns, to see how the shell expands them. You can construct other commands using *echo*. The command shown below tests a pattern, and the history operator !$ repeats it:

```
% echo pattern          Test a pattern
% more !$               Pass the pattern to another command
```

This technique is particularly valuable for dangerous commands like *rm*, which can remove too many files if a pattern matches more names than you intend. By using *echo* to test a pattern first, you're in no danger of removing anything erroneously.

You can use *echo* in conjunction with history operators to refine a pattern that's incorrect, but close to what you want:

```
% echo *.tar*                           Try pattern
argyle.tar blrgle.tar.gz oot-greet.tar
% ^r*^r                                 Change pattern to *.tar and try again
echo *.tar                              Shell echoes new command
argyle.tar oot-greet.tar
% rm !$                                 Use pattern to remove the file
rm *.tar                                Shell echoes new command
```

In *tcsh*, you can use the command editor's *list-glob* command to see what a file-name pattern expands to. *list-glob* (bound to CTRL-X g) displays matches for the filename pattern immediately to the left of the cursor, as shown below:

```
% echo *.tar*█                          Type pattern, then CTRL-X g
argyle.tar blrgle.tar.gz oot-greet.tar  tcsh displays matching filenames...
% echo *.tar*█                          ...then redisplays the command
```

Using { } To Generate Arguments

Filename patterns can be used only to refer to existing files. If you need to specify names, regardless of whether or not the files exist (usually to create new files or give new names to existing ones), use the shell's { } construct.

Suppose that you want to create a set of new directories with names *Project1* through *Project5*. You can't use a pattern like `Project[1-5]`, because that pattern works only for existing names, as shown below:

```
% mkdir Project[1-5]
mkdir: No match.
```

You could type out every name:

```
% mkdir Project1 Project2 Project3 Project4 Project5
```

But that's tedious. It's much easier to use { } to generate arguments:

```
% mkdir Project{1,2,3,4,5}
```

The shell looks at the comma-separated strings between the braces and creates one argument for each string.

You can use { } to mix references to existing and nonexisting files. The following command renames *chapter8* to *chapter9*, even if *chapter9* doesn't exist:

```
% mv chapter{8,9}
```

To rename the file to its original name, do the following:

```
% mv chapter{9,8}
```

Any or all of the strings within { } can be empty. Therefore, the following pairs of commands are equivalent:

- Compare *document.old* and *document* for differences:

```
% diff document.old document
% diff document{.old,}
```

- Make a backup copy of *program.c* named *progam.c.bak*:

```
% cp program.c program.c.bak
% cp program.c{,.bak}
```

- Encode a file *utilities-3.04.tar.Z* into *junk*:

```
% uuencode utilities-3.04.tar.Z utilities-3.04.tar.Z > junk
% uuencode utilities-3.04.tar.Z{,} > junk
```

{ } might not be as intuitive as the pattern operators, since it can be used to specify non-existent files (or even arguments that don't refer to files at all), but you'll find that it's quite useful. Again, *echo* is helpful while you learn the construct, just as it is when you're learning to use filename patterns. The following examples use *echo* to demonstrate other aspects of the way in which { } works.

{ } need not appear at the end of an argument:

```
% echo {y,d}abba doo, {w,bl}inken nod, t{i,a}c toe
yabba dabba doo, winken blinken nod, tic tac toe
```

You can use { } more than once in an argument:

```
% echo {a,b,c}{0,1,2}
a0 a1 a2 b0 b1 b2 c0 c1 c2
```

You can even nest { }:

```
% echo part{a,b{1,2,3},c}
parta partb1 partb2 partb3 partc
```

To include a special character or a comma inside { }, precede it with a backslash:

```
% echo "pease porridge "{hot\,,cold\!}
pease porridge hot, pease porridge cold!
```

Argument expansion with { } occurs in the order you specify. If you have two files named *parta* and *partb*, the following commands are different. The first command receives the files that match the pattern in alphabetical order, because pattern matches are sorted before being substituted into the command line. The second command receives the files in the order named:

```
% echo part[ba]
parta partb
% echo part{b,a}
partb parta
```

Directory Naming Shorthand

Both *csh* and *tcsh* provide a shorthand notation for referring to user account home directories, and *tcsh* provides a shorthand for referring to entries in your directory stack.

Referring to Home Directories Using ~name

The shell interprets ~ or *~name* at the beginning of pathnames to mean your home directory, or the home directory for user *name*. These shortcuts give you a quick way to refer to any user's home directory, without typing (or even knowing) the actual pathname. Thus, if I want to see what files *carl* has in his home directory, I don't have to know where that directory is; I just type the following command:

```
% ls ~carl
```

I can edit my *calendar* file, no matter where I am, with the following command:

```
% vi ~/calendar
```

Suppose I'm located deep in my directory hierarchy, and I want to copy a file *intro.ms.new* from my *Thesis* directory to my current directory. I want to avoid specifying long absolute or relative paths to the file like those shown below:

```
% cp /usr/staff/dubois/Thesis/intro.ms.new .          (or)
% cp ../../../../Thesis/intro.ms.new .
```

Neither of these alternatives is attractive. The absolute path is long, and when typing a relative path it's easy to go up too few or too many levels by mistake. It's a lot simpler to type this, instead:

```
% cp ~/Thesis/intro.ms.new .
```

If *intro.ms.new* is located under someone else's account, I can easily get a copy of the file by using the following command:

```
% cp ~colleen/Thesis/intro.ms.new .
```

Referring to Directory Stack Entries Using =n

In *tcsh*, entries from the directory stack can be used to construct command arguments. If you begin an argument with *=n*, it's equivalent to typing out the name of entry *n* from your directory stack. This allows you to refer easily to those directories, and their files, without typing out long pathnames. This use of the directory stack is discussed further in Chapter 13, *Navigating the File System*.

10

Filename and Programmed Completion

The shell can do some typing for you, by performing filename completion. You type a filename prefix, hit a special key, and the shell supplies the rest of the filename.

csh and *tcsh* both have built-in filename completion. *tcsh* has command-name completion as well, and allows you to program your own types of completion on a per-command basis (when the built in completion facilities don't perform as needed). For example, you can tell *tcsh* to complete an argument to *mail* as a username rather than as a filename, or to complete arguments to *cd* using only directory names.

Using Built-In Filename Completion

In *tcsh*, filename completion is always active: just type the first part of a name and hit the TAB key. *tcsh* determines which name matches the prefix, and types out the rest for you. If you have a file named *experiment.data*, you can type its name quickly, like this:

```
% more ex█                          Type the prefix ex, then hit TAB
% more experiment.data█             Shell types rest of name
```

In *csh*, you hit ESC rather than TAB after typing the prefix. Also, filename completion isn't active unless you set the *filec* shell variable.[*] Therefore, put the following command in your ~/.cshrc file first:

---

[*] Some versions of *csh* use the variable *complete* instead of *filec*, and *csh* on some systems (ULTRIX 3.1, for example) doesn't do filename completion at all (a reason to switch to *tcsh*).

```
set filec
```

If a prefix matches more than one filename, the shell cannot tell which file you really want. Completion is still valuable because the shell supplies as much of the name as is common to the possible matches, then beeps to alert you to the ambiguity. Suppose you have files named *experiment1.data*, *experiment2.data*, and *experiment3.data*. If you type **ex** and hit the completion key, the shell will supply periment:

```
% more ex█                          Type prefix, then hit completion key
% more experiment█                  Shell does partial completion and beeps
```

To finish the job, type 1, 2, or 3 to indicate which file you want, and hit the completion key again. The shell adds .data, and you're done.

tcsh adds a space when it completes the name of a plain file, and a slash (/) after directory names. The extra character provides a visual indicator of successful completion. Also, the space is useful because you don't have to type it yourself if you're typing another argument, and is otherwise harmless. The slash is helpful if you're typing a long pathname, because you can complete each component of the name without typing a separating slash after each one. Suppose I want to execute the following command:

```
% cd ~/Papers/References/Books
```

In *tcsh*, I might be able to specify the directory pathname with as little typing as ~/P TAB R TAB B TAB.

csh adds nothing to completed filenames. You can still complete multiple pathname components, but you have to type the slashes yourself. If you'd prefer *tcsh* to work that way, too, put the following in your *~/.cshrc* file:

```
unset addsuffix
```

If a word to be completed begins with a ~, both *csh* and *tcsh* complete it as a home directory reference of the form ~*name*:

```
% cd ~du█                           Type home directory prefix, then hit completion key
% cd ~dubois█                       Shell completes directory reference
```

(*tcsh* also adds a slash because ~*dubois* refers to a directory.)

Displaying Completion Matches

The shell beeps when you attempt completion of an ambiguous prefix. However, if you can't remember which names match the prefix, there's no need to cancel the command and run *ls*. Just type CTRL-D; the shell prints an *ls* style display of the matching names, and then reprints the command line.[*] You can continue entering the command where you left off:

```
% more dat94█                          Type prefix, then hit CTRL-D
dat94.01    dat94.03    dat94.05       Shell displays matching filenames...
dat94.02    dat94.04
% more dat94█                          ...then redisplays command line
```

Match listing works for home directory references as well. To see which account names begin with *d*, try this:

```
% echo ~d█                             Type prefix, then hit CTRL-D
daemon   dan      david    deb      debby     dick     donna    dubois
dale     daniel   dc       debbie   deutsch   dom      dorder   dws
% echo ~d█
```

If a completion fails because there are no matches, CTRL-D won't show anything, as shown below:

```
% echo xyz█                            Type prefix, then hit CTRL-D
% echo xyz█                            No matches
```

Narrowing the Scope of Completion Matches

To ignore names with certain suffixes, set the *fignore* shell variable. This feature can rule out whole classes of filenames, and more often results in successful completions by reducing the number of candidate names. For example, if you're not interested in using names of object files or backup files to form completions, add the following command to your `~/.cshrc` file:

```
set fignore = ( .o .bak \~ )   Don't use filenames ending in .o, .bak, or ~ for matching
```

In this example, the ~ is preceded by a backslash, so the shell doesn't immediately expand it to the pathname of your home directory.

fignore itself is ignored under the following circumstances:

- If a completion is matched by a single name, the name is used even if its suffix is listed in *fignore*.

- When you type CTRL-D to list matches for a prefix, all matches are displayed, whether or not *fignore* is set.

- If you're using a programmed completion (described later in this chapter) with a completion rule that includes its own criterion about which names to ignore, that criterion takes precedence over *fignore*.

---

[*] Actually, the display looks more like the output of *ls −F*. *csh* and *tcsh* both indicate executable files or directories with a * or / after the name. *tcsh* also indicates sockets, block and character devices, symbolic links, and FIFO files using =, #, %, @, and |.

Other Types of Completions

tcsh does completion and match listing for some words that *csh* does not:

- Words at the beginning of the command line or after |, &, ;, ||, or && are assumed to be command names. *tcsh* completes them as such by looking for a match not only in your current directory, but also in the directories in your command search path (i.e., directories named in your *path* shell variable).

- Words beginning with $ are completed as variable names. If *version* is your only variable name beginning with v, you can type $v and hit TAB, and *tcsh* completes it to $version.

  If *tcsh* can determine that you've typed a variable's entire name (because you've typed a slash after it), completions are done the same way as if you'd typed the variable's value:

  ```
  % set cron = /usr/spool/cron    Assign value to variable
  % ls $cron/c█                   Type variable reference and /c, and hit TAB
  % ls $cron/crontabs█            tcsh determines that you mean /usr/spool/cron/crontabs
  ```

- Words beginning with =*n* are interpreted as if they begin with the value of directory stack entry *n*.[*] Suppose your stack looks like this:

  ```
  % dirs -v
  0    ~/src/myprog
  1    /usr/include
  2    /usr/local/include
  ```

  Then, in the example below, the shell interprets =1 as */usr/include*, and completes me to memory.h, which is a file in that directory:

  ```
  % more =1/me█                   Type prefix, then hit TAB
  % more =1/memory.h█
  ```

Listing Completion Matches Automatically

When more than one completion is possible, *tcsh* can automatically display matches. Set the *autolist* shell variable in your *~/.cshrc* file using one of the commands shown below:

```
set autolist
set autolist = ambiguous
```

The first form results in match listing for any completion failure. The second form results in automatic listing only if multiple matches are possible, and if the completion adds no new characters to the name to be matched.

If you commonly work in directories that contain lots of files, or that are network-mounted over a slow link, match listing with CTRL-D can be slow and/or produce

---

* See Chapter 13, *Navigating the File System*, for more information about the directory stack.

a lot of output. Setting *autolist* can make this problem worse. However, *tcsh* provides some shell variables for tailoring match-listing behavior:

- Set *listmax* to the maximum number of matches *tcsh* should list. If there are more matches, *tcsh* asks for confirmation before proceeding.

- Set *listmaxrows* to the maximum number of rows of matches *tcsh* should list. If there are more rows, *tcsh* asks for confirmation before proceeding.

Completion and the tcsh Command Editor

In *tcsh*, TAB and CTRL–D perform completion and match listing as part of the command editor. You can use other command editor functions to complement standard completion behavior. The sections below discuss a few of the possibilities.

Stepping through possible completions

The *complete-word-fwd* editor command replaces the prefix to the left of the cursor with the first of those words that match the prefix. If the command is repeated, the current word is replaced with successive matches. This allows you to step through the list of completions until you find the one you want. If you reach the end of the list, *tcsh* beeps and replaces the current word with the original prefix. *complete-word-back* works similarly, but steps through the matching words in reverse order.

Unfortunately, these commands aren't bound to any keys by default, so you must set up your own bindings. For example, if you want to use the left arrow and right arrow keys to step through the completions backward and forward, you can put the following commands in your `~/.cshrc` file:

```
bindkey -k left complete-word-back
bindkey -k right complete-word-fwd
```

See Chapter 7, *The tcsh Command-Line Editor*, for more information on creating your own key bindings.

Completion in mid-command

The *tcsh* command editor allows you to move the cursor to any point in the current command line.[*] Thus, although completion is most often used with the cursor at the end of the line, in *tcsh* you have the option of performing completions in mid-line. Only the prefix to the left of the cursor is completed, so if the cursor is in the middle of a word, some of the characters following it may become extraneous and need to be deleted after you perform a completion.

CTRL–D lists prefix matches in mid-command when used with the *vi* bindings, but not with the *emacs* bindings.

---

[*] See Chapter 7 for information about command editing.

Completion and filename patterns

Filename completion doesn't work for words that contain pattern characters or { }, but such words can be expanded in *tcsh* with the command editor's *expand-glob* command. *expand-glob* is bound to CTRL-X * in *emacs* mode and to * in *vi* command mode. Thus, if you edit commands using the *emacs* bindings, you can expand a pattern, like this:

```
% more results.*█                          Type pattern, then CTRL-X *
% more results.expt1 results.expt2 results.expt3█    tcsh expands the pattern
```

If you want to see which names match the pattern without expanding the command line, use the *list-glob* command (CTRL-X g for either set of bindings). For example, you can use *list-glob* to check a pattern you're specifying in an *rm* command, and determine if the command will remove the intended files. If not, you can edit the pattern.

Like completion, the *expand-glob* and *list-glob* editor commands work at any point in the command line, expanding or listing expansions of the word immediately to the left of the cursor.

Programmed Completions

tcsh has programmed completions, a facility that allows you to associate specific types of completion with individual commands. This feature is useful when the built-in completion behavior, described in the preceding sections, doesn't complete words the way you want. For example, you might want to complete an argument as a username, or complete some arguments differently than others, or determine how to complete a word based on what the preceding word looks like.

Programmed completions are triggered the same way as regular completions (TAB completes a word and CTRL-D displays possible matches), but you specify their behavior using the *complete* command. The syntax of *complete* is rather cumbersome, so we'll wait until later in the chapter to examine it more closely. First, we'll look at some examples of *complete* to get a general idea of how it works. (You can find many more programmed completion examples in the file *complete.tcsh* included with the *tcsh* source distribution. It provides ready-made completions that you can borrow, and it will give you ideas for creating your own. If you don't have that distribution, Appendix C, *Other Sources of Information*, indicates how to obtain *complete.tcsh* separately.)

Programmed completions are best placed in your *˜/.cshrc* file so they're available to your login shell as well as any subshells.* Don't put a *complete* command in *˜/.cshrc* until you've verified that it works correctly. Define the completion at the command line first, and then test it. If the completion doesn't seem to be working

---

* *complete* is a *tcsh*-specific command, so you should protect it from *csh* by using the instructions in Chapter 4, *The Shell Startup Files*.

correctly, use one of these commands to determine whether the shell is interpreting your definition the way you expect:

```
% complete              Display all completion definitions
% complete name         Display completion definition for command name
```

Let's consider some examples. Suppose you want to improve the efficiency of completions for *cd* by ignoring non-directories. You can do so with the following *complete* command:

```
complete cd 'p/1/d/'
```

The first argument, cd, names the command to perform completions for. The complicated argument following cd is a completion rule: p indicates that the rule applies to a word in a given position, 1 specifies which position (in this example, the first word following the command name), and d defines how to complete the word (as a directory name).

This completion helps you because non-directory files are irrelevant for location changes. By excluding them from consideration when completing the argument to *cd*, you're more likely to get a unique match (and thus a successful completion). You also get a smaller list of names that's easier to look through when you type CTRL-D to get a list of matches. This is similar to setting *fignore*, except that names are excluded based on the type of file they represent, rather than what they look like.

Other position specifiers can be used. For example, *rmdir* takes directory arguments like *cd* does. However, *rmdir* allows you to name multiple directories to be removed, so a completion rule that applies to any argument is more appropriate. You can use the * position specifier ("all positions") to write such a rule:

```
complete rmdir 'p/*/d/'
```

The position specifiers that are available are shown in Table 10-1 (1 and * are the most commonly used).

Programmed completions aren't limited to filenames, so they can be used for commands like those shown below, all of which take non-filename arguments:

```
% printenv name         Display value of environment variable name
% alias name            Display definition of alias name
% mail name             Send mail to user name
```

You can set up appropriate completions for each of the commands to help you type their arguments more easily (*mail* allows you to specify multiple recipients, hence the use of * for the position specifier):

```
complete printenv 'p/1/e/'     Complete argument with environment variable name
complete alias 'p/1/a/'        Complete argument with alias name
complete mail 'p/*/u/'         Complete arguments with usernames
```

The word types you can use for completions are shown in Table 10-2. Most of these types are predefined, but you can also specify your own list of words to use for completing arguments. Suppose you frequently connect to a set of machines using *ftp*. You can make it easier to type their names as shown below, where the completion list is given as a set of space-separated words between parentheses:

```
complete ftp 'p/1/(ftp.uu.net wuarchive.wustl.edu prep.ai.mit.edu info.cern.ch)/'
```

If you're connecting to a site that isn't listed, you have to type out its whole name. But you still save yourself typing to the extent that the list contains the machines you connect to most often. This example illustrates that programmed completions can be useful even if they don't cover every possible argument.

So far, the examples have used p-type completion rules, which apply to words based on their positions in the command line. You can also write completion rules that are triggered by words whose leftmost part matches a pattern. Pattern-based rules can complete the matched word, the next word after it, or the word after that.

To demonstrate pattern-based rules, let's look at the *find* command. *find* has a lot of flags. A completion rule can help you type them:

```
complete find 'c/-/(user group type name print exec mtime fstype perm size)/'
```

The c that begins the rule indicates that it completes the "current word," i.e., the word matched by the pattern (a dash). The rule completes any word that begins with – using one of the words from the parenthesized list:

```
% find . -g█              Type flag prefix, then hit TAB
% find . -group█          tcsh completes flag name
```

Because prefix match listing works with programmed completions, the *find* completion rule does more than help you complete the flag names. It also provides a handy way to obtain help if, like me, you can't always remember the various flag names. Just type a dash and hit CTRL–D to see a list of flags, as shown below:

```
% find . -█                           Type dash, then hit CTRL–D
exec    group   name    print   type  tcsh displays flag names
fstype  mtime   perm    size    user
% find . -█
```

In this example, the completion rule serves as a memory aid by providing a form of online assistance.

n-type pattern rules match one word and complete the next one. They're especially useful for completing a word that follows a particular flag. For example, the *find* completion command can be improved by adding a few rules to complete the words that follow the *–user* and *–group* flags as user and group names:

```
complete find \
        'c/-/(user group type name print exec mtime fstype perm size)/' \
        'n/-user/u/' \
        'n/-group/g/'
```

The command above illustrates that *complete* can take multiple completion rules. Note also the use of backslashes to continue the command over multiple lines. This convention improves the readability of long *complete* commands.

You can mix position-based and pattern-based rules in a *complete* command. The first argument to *find* is a directory, so the argument can be completed by adding a p-type rule:

```
complete find \
        'p/1/d/' \
        'c/-/(user group type name print exec mtime fstype perm size)/' \
        'n/-user/u/' \
        'n/-group/g/'
```

The string matched by pattern-based rules need not begin with a dash. The *dd* command accepts if=*file* and of=*file* arguments to specify the input and output files. The following *complete* command allows you to match words that begin with a prefix of if= or of=, then complete whatever follows the prefix as a filename:

```
complete dd 'c/[io]f=/f/'
```

The command shows how filename pattern operators can be used in a completion rule—the pattern matches both if= and of=.

When a completion rule or set of rules can be applied to several commands, you need not write several individual *complete* commands like this:

```
complete cd 'p/1/d/'
complete pushd 'p/1/d/'
```

Instead, you can specify all the command names in a brace list:

```
complete {cd,pushd} 'p/1/d/'
```

Syntax of the complete Command

Now that we've seen some examples, we're in a better position to consider the syntax of the *complete* command more systematically. *complete* has several elements because it needs several kinds of information:

```
complete command word/pattern/list/suffix
```

command is the name of the command to be completed. The argument following it is the rule describing how to complete words for the command.

Completion rules consist of the following parts:

- *word* and *pattern* describe how to choose words to be completed.

- *list* specifies the word list from which to choose completions, e.g., names of files, users, groups, or variables. Alternatively, you can supply your own list of words or run a command to generate them.

- *suffix* lets you specify a suffix other than space or slash to be added to a successful completion. *suffix* is optional, but should be a single character if given. To specify explicitly that no suffix at all should be added, include another slash immediately following the one after *list*.

A completion rule should be quoted if it contains characters like * that are special to the shell. I find it easiest simply to quote all my rules.

The parts of a completion rule are usually delimited with slashes, but you can use a different character, as shown below:

```
complete man 'p,*,c,'          Comma delimiter
complete cd 'p:1:d:'           Colon delimiter
```

Selecting the Word To Be Completed

The *word* and *pattern* values work together to determine which word or words the completion rule applies to. You can apply a completion rule by position or by pattern match.

Position-based word selection

For position-based rules, *word* is p and *pattern* specifies word positions as shown in Table 10–1. The pattern * means any position, so a p-type rule with a position specifier of * applies to any of a command's arguments.

Table 10–1: Word Position Specifiers for p-Type Completion Rules

Position	Description
n	Word *n*
m–n	Words *m* through *n*
*m**	Words *m* through last word
*	All words

Pattern-based word selection

If *word* is c, n, C, or N, the rule is pattern-based and is triggered by any word whose initial part matches *pattern*. The pattern can be a literal string or it can contain pattern matching operators (*, ?, [ ]) or the { } construct.

Pattern rule *word* specifiers perform completions as described below:

c   c-type rules complete the current word (the word matched by *pattern*). Only the part of the word following the initial string matched by *pattern* is used as the prefix to be completed. This specifier allows you to match the leading part of a word, skip over that part, and complete the rest of the word.

n   n-type rules complete the next word after the word matched by *pattern*. These rules are often used to match a particular flag and complete the word that follows it.

C   Like c, except that the entire word, including the part matched by *pattern*, is used as the prefix to be completed.

N   Like n, but the rule completes the second word after the word matched by *pattern*.

c-type and n-type rules are used a lot. C-type and N-type rules are used less frequently.

Completing the Selected Word

The *list* part of a completion rule specifies what kind of completion to perform—that is, what type of word you want to end up with. The various *list* specifiers are shown in Table 10–2. Most are single character codes designating an attribute that completions must satisfy (for example, e indicates that the word must be chosen from the list of variables currently defined in your environment). The last three specifiers provide various ways of indicating an arbitrary list of words from which to choose.

Table 10–2: Completion Rule Word List Types

List	Description
a	Alias names
b	Key binding names (command-line editor commands)
c	Command names
d	Directory names
e	Environment variable names
f	Filenames (any type, including directory names)
g	Group names
j	Jobs names
l	Resource limit names
n	Null list (suppresses completion)
s	Shell variable names
S	Signal names
t	Plain text filenames (actually, any non-directory)
v	Variable names (any type)
u	User names
X	Command names for which completions have been defined
x	Explain; like n, but print a message when you type CTRL-D
C, D, F, T	Like c, d, f, t, but select completion from a given directory
(*list*)	Select completion from words in the given list

Table 10–2: Completion Rule Word List Types (continued)

List	Description
$variable	Select completion from words in the value of the variable
`command`	Select completion from words in the output of the command

Restricting the set of completion words

The attribute-based word list specifiers limit completions to the type of word indicated, but you have the option of providing an additional criterion to further narrow the allowable choices. To do this, specify the list in *list:restrict* form, where *restrict* is a filename pattern. Only members of *list* that match the pattern are candidates for the completion. *restrict* can include pattern-matching operators (*, ?, []) or the {} construct. The following commands specify that *uncompress* arguments are completed using only filenames ending in .Z, whereas *gunzip* arguments are completed using filenames ending in .z, .gz, or .Z:

```
complete uncompress 'p/*/f:*.Z/'
complete gunzip 'p/*/f:*.{z,gz,Z}/'
```

The pattern can also begin with ^ to reverse the sense of the match. For example, it's unlikely that you'll use *vi* to edit core dumps, object (.o) files, or library (.a) files. The following *complete* command restricts filename completion to exclude those files:

```
complete vi 'p/*/f:^{core,*.[oa]}/'
```

restrict is similar in function to the *fignore* shell variable, which is used with built-in completions to ignore names with certain suffixes. However, *restrict* differs from *fignore* in several ways:

- *restrict* has higher priority; *fignore* is ignored by rules that specify a restriction.

- *restrict* selects or excludes names based on arbitrary patterns. This is more general than *fignore*, which excludes names based only on the suffix.

- Restrictions are not ignored (as with *fignore*) when there is only one match for the word to be completed. If only one word of the required type matches the prefix, the word is not used unless it satisfies the restriction pattern.

- Similarly, restrictions are not ignored (as with *fignore*) when you type CTRL–D to list matches for the word to be completed.

Choosing completions from a given directory

The C, D, F, and T word list types are like the corresponding c, d, f, and t types except that they must be followed by a :*path* designator that specifies a directory. Completions are formed from the commands, directories, files, or plain files located in the given directory. For example, I can invoke the *elm* mailer, as shown below, to read mail from *file* rather than from my system mailbox:

```
% elm -f file
```

If *file* is specified with a leading =, e.g., *=xyz*, *elm* assumes that the file *xyz* is located in my private mail directory. *elm* provides this syntax as a handy shortcut allowing me to read files from my home directory easily, regardless of my location. Unfortunately, the leading = also defeats built-in filename completion. To circumvent such problems, I can use a programmed completion to tell *tcsh* to treat words beginning with = as though they really begin with the pathname to my mail directory, as shown below:

```
complete elm 'c@=@F:/usr/staff/dubois/Mail@'
```

The completion rule uses a non-slash delimiter (@ in this case) because the directory name contains slashes.

Displaying a message instead of listing matches

The **x** (explain) word list type suppresses completion like **n** but takes a **:*message*** designator that defines a message that will be displayed if you try to list matches for a prefix. For example, **x** can be used to present the information that *sleep* takes a sleep time in seconds as shown below:

```
complete sleep 'p/*/x:specify one argument indicating a sleep time in seconds/'
```

Supplying your own completion word list

If none of the single-character *list* types describe the set of words that you want to use for a completion rule, provide your own list. You can do so via three methods: by providing an explicit set of words between parentheses, by listing the words in a variable, or by running a command that produces the words.

Suppose that you typically use *rlogin* to connect to one of a particular set of hosts using one of a given set of login names, as shown below:

```
% rlogin host -l name
```

Because the machine name is the first argument and the login name follows the *-l* flag, you can write an *rlogin* completion as follows:

```
complete rlogin \
        'p/1/(sidewinder cottonmouth massasauga diamondback)/' \
        'n/-l/(almanac ftpmail postgres majordom)/'
```

You can then complete the machine name as well as the username, as shown below:

```
% rlogin s                Type hostname prefix, then hit TAB
% rlogin sidewinder       tcsh completes the hostname
```

```
% rlogin sidewinder -l m█            Type -l and username prefix, then hit TAB
% rlogin sidewinder -l majordom█     tcsh completes the username
```

Now, suppose that you want to use the same hostname list for other networking commands like *telnet* or *rsh*.* Here is one method of doing so:

```
complete rlogin \
        'p/1/(sidewinder cottonmouth massasauga diamondback)/' \
        'n/-l/(almanac ftpmail postgres majordom)/'
complete telnet 'p/1/(sidewinder cottonmouth massasauga diamondback)/'
complete rsh 'p/1/(sidewinder cottonmouth massasauga diamondback)/'
```

However, if you want to change the list of machine names later, you must change it in three places. You could, instead, assign the list of words to a variable and share the list among completion rules by referring to the variable:

```
set machines = (sidewinder cottonmouth massasauga diamondback)
complete rlogin \
        'p/1/$machines/' \
        'n/-l/(almanac ftpmail postgres majordom)/'
complete telnet 'p/1/$machines/'
complete rsh 'p/1/$machines/'
```

Now you only have to change the variable's value to change the list everywhere it's used.

If the word list specifier is a shell command inside backquotes, completions are chosen from the set of words generated by that command. Suppose you want to use *talk* to converse with other people on your machine. You could tell *tcsh* to complete the *talk* argument as a username, as shown below:

```
complete talk 'p/1/u/'
```

However, that rule might complete a word with the name of a user who is not even logged in. To use only the names of active users, run a command that determines the set of active users, as shown below:

```
complete talk 'p/1/`who|cut -c1-8|sort -u`/'
```

A backquoted command in a completion rule can be arbitrarily simple or complex. However, it's best if the command runs reasonably quickly, since it's executed each time the rule is selected when you attempt a completion. If the command is slow, the completion will be slow, too, and frustrating.

Adding a suffix to the completed word

tcsh completion normally adds a slash to completed directory names and a space to filenames and other types of words. You can specify a different suffix character, or even no suffix at all. The suffix character is given after the delimiter that follows the word list type.

---

* *rsh* is called *remsh* on some systems.

The *finger* command typically takes an argument of the form *user@host*, which is difficult to complete in one operation. However, you can complete the first part of the argument as a username and supply a suffix of @ to make typing the hostname easier:

```
complete finger 'p/*/u/@'
```

You can also suppress suffix addition completely by adding another delimiter immediately following the one after the word list type. For example, World Wide Web browsers such as *lynx* or *xmosaic* can be executed with an argument specifying the universal resource locator (URL) for the information you want to access. The rule below completes the resource part of a URL and suppresses the space that normally would be added:

```
complete {lynx,xmosaic} 'p#1#(http:// ftp:// gopher:// wais:// mailto: news:)##'
```

That way you don't have to back up over a space before typing the rest of the argument.

Specifying Multiple Completion Rules

Multiple completion rules allow you to complete some arguments differently than others, but you should keep the following points in mind.

First, all completion rules for a given command must be given on the same *complete* command. Do not issue a separate *complete* command for each rule. If you try to specify *rlogin* completion for the hostname and login name arguments as shown below, your attempt will fail. The second command simply replaces the first:

```
complete rlogin 'p/1/(sidewinder cottonmouth massasauga diamondback)/'
complete rlogin 'n/-l/(almanac ftpmail postgres majordom)/'
```

Second, it is important to be careful about the order in which you specify multiple completion rules. Rules are tried left to right until one is found that applies. Consider the *complete* command for *mail* shown below. The intent is to complete the argument following *–f* as a filename, suppress completion of the argument following *–s*, and complete any other argument as a username:

```
complete mail 'p/*/u/' 'n/-f/f/' 'n/-s/n/'
```

However, the completion does not work as intended. The p-type rule is tried first, and applies to all words. Therefore, the n-type rules are never used. The command should be changed and specified as follows:

```
complete mail 'n/-f/f/' 'n/-s/n/' 'p/*/u/'
```

A good rule of thumb is that any rule applying to all words should be listed last so that other rules have a chance to be tried.

Displaying and Removing Programmed Completions

To display all completions or a specific completion, use the commands shown below:

```
% complete                        Display all completions
% complete command                Display completions for command
```

If a completion does not work as it should, try displaying its definition. You may find that *tcsh* did not interpret your definition as you expected.

To remove a completion, use *uncomplete*:

```
% uncomplete command              Remove completion for command
% uncomplete *                    Remove all completions
```

When Programmed Completions Do Not Apply

There are various circumstances under which programmed completions do not apply and for which *tcsh* reverts to its regular built-in completion behavior:

- A regular completion is done when you try to complete a word of a command for which a programmed completion has been defined and none of the completion rules apply. This rule makes better sense if you consider, for example, a case in which you are trying to complete word 2 and have supplied a rule only for word 1. However, you may find regular completions being done unexpectedly. The usual symptom of such occurrences is that a word unexpectedly completes as a filename, that was to be excluded. When such instances happen, check your completion rules, because they probably aren't set up correctly.

- Words beginning with $ or ~ are completed to $*variable* or ~*name* references, and any programmed completions are ignored. However, if $*variable* or ~*name* is followed by a slash, *tcsh* knows the whole variable or username has been supplied and can tell which directory you're referring to. At that point, programmed completions apply again.

- You can override programmed completions and do a regular completion or match listing by typing CTRL-X TAB or CTRL-X CTRL-D, rather than TAB or CTRL-D.

11

Quoting and Special Characters

This chapter describes how to quote special characters when you need to type them in a command line, as happens when a filename contains a space, &, or *.

Special Characters

The shell normally assigns special meanings to several characters (see Table 11-1). As you gain experience with the shell and learn these meanings, the fact that these characters are not interpreted literally tends to become a fact you take for granted. For example, after you know that & signifies background execution and begin to use it accordingly, the convention becomes second-nature—part of your repertoire of shell-using skills.

However, this set of skills is incomplete unless you also know how to use special characters literally, because sometimes you need to turn off their special meanings. Suppose you have a file named *Budget-R&D*. That's a perfectly legal filename. However, since the name contains a & character, if you try to use the name without turning off the &, the character will trigger a flurry of activity and multiple error messages:

```
% wc Budget-R&D
[1] 10413
wc: Budget-R: No such file or directory.
[1]    Exit 2              wc Budget-R
D: Command not found.
```

The shell provides a quoting mechanism for situations like the one described above, which allows you to use special characters like ordinary characters by turning off their special meanings. The rest of this chapter describes the quoting rules and how to take advantage of them.

Table 11-1: Characters That Are Special to the Shell

Character(s)	Description
* ? [ ] ^ { } ~	Filename pattern matching and expansion
$	Variable reference
|	Pipe
< >	Input and output redirection
! ^	History reference and quick substitution
&	Background execution
;	Command separator
SPACE	Argument separator
TAB	Filename completion (*tcsh*)
ESC	Filename completion (*csh*)
(...)	Subshell execution
`...`	Command substitution
\ ' "	Quote characters

The Shell's Quote Characters

Four characters are used for quoting. They turn off (or "escape") special character meanings:

- A backslash (\) turns off the special meaning of the following character.

- Single quotes ('...') turn off the special meaning of the characters between the quotes, except that ! *event* still indicates history substitution.

- Double quotes ("...") turn off the special meaning of the characters between the quotes, except that ! *event*, $*var*, and `*cmd*` still indicate history, variable, and command substitution. (You can think of double quotes as being "weaker" than single quotes because they turn off fewer special characters.)

- The lnext ("literal next") character turns off the special meaning of the following character.[*] This character can be used with special characters that are otherwise interpreted as soon as they are typed. For example, in *tcsh* a TAB triggers filename completion; therefore, you cannot type a literal TAB unless you precede it with CTRL-V.

Quoting the Quote Characters

The quote characters can be used to type literal quote characters, not simply to turn off the special meaning of other special characters.

---

[*] The lnext character is usually CTRL-V. See Chapter 5, *Setting Up Your Terminal*, for more information.

Backslash and CTRL-V quote themselves. In other words, \\ produces \ and CTRL-V CTRL-V produces CTRL-V.

Single and double quote marks quote each other:

```
% echo "'" '"'
' "
```

Backslash quotes quote marks:

```
% echo \' \"
' "
```

And quote marks quote backslashes:

```
% echo '\' "\"
\ \
```

The following sections describe several practical methods of using the quote characters.

Referring to Files with Problematic Names

Occasionally, you may find yourself in possession of a file with a name containing special characters such as SPACE or ? or !, or perhaps even CTRL-H. You're not likely to create such names inadvertently from the command line, but it's relatively easy to do so in other circumstances. For example, you might discover, after saving an item in a *gopher* session, that you own a file with a lovely name like this:

```
<<** New Items! (READ THIS!!) **>>
```

Such a name can occur because, when you save an item to a file, some *gopher* clients suggest a default name that is the same as the item's title in the current menu.

Or, you might use FTP to grab files from a machine that is running an operating system with different filename conventions than UNIX. If the files you are retrieving have names containing characters the shell considers special, and your FTP program doesn't map them onto ordinary characters, you end up with files that are hard to refer to.

Usually, the best method for working with a difficult filename is to change the name immediately to something easier to use. Or, you might consider deleting the file, because often files that have ornery names were created accidentally and are unwanted.

Suppose that we have some files with names that contain various special characters, as shown below:

```
abc;1
Home Work
!abc
```

```
!abc and def
My Summer Vacation (Part 2)
RED CTRL-H ADME
<<** New Items! (READ THIS!!) **>>
```

To work with difficult filenames like those shown above, you usually have several options:

- Use filename completion and let the shell quote the special characters (*tcsh* only)

- Use a pattern and let the shell supply the filename

- Quote the special characters yourself

Let's explore these options in order, in the section that follows.

Typing Difficult Filenames Using Filename Completion

When *tcsh* completes a name, it puts a backslash in front of any special characters to quote them. As a result, if you are using *tcsh* and you can easily specify a unique prefix of a filename, letting *tcsh* complete the name is often the easiest way of typing it:

```
% rm Home█                                   Type filename prefix
% rm Home\ Work█                             Hit TAB; tcsh supplies rest of name

% mv My█                                     Type filename prefix
% mv My\ Summer\ Vacation\ \(Part\ 2\)█      Hit TAB; tcsh supplies rest of name
% mv My\ Summer\ Vacation\ \(Part\ 2\) my-vac-2█   Type rest of command
```

csh can complete filenames, too, but it does not escape special characters. Therefore, csh is unsuitable for typing difficult filenames in this manner.

Typing Difficult Filenames Using Filename Patterns

If a filename begins with special characters, you can have difficulty in typing a unique prefix to use for filename completion. For example, the name below begins with five special characters:

```
<<** New Items! (READ THIS!!) **>>
```

Usually, you will find that filename patterns make it easier to refer to such names. If you can find a pattern that uniquely matches the name, the shell figures out which file you want to select. To use this technique, run *echo* to verify that a pattern matches only the file in question, then use the pattern to rename the file:

```
% echo *Items*                               Try the pattern
<<** New Items! (READ THIS!!) **>>           Yes, it matches just this one name
% mv *Items* NewItems                        Rename the file using the pattern
```

If the *echo* command shows more than one match, try a different pattern. When you have a suitable pattern, use it to rename the file.

If you are trying to get rid of a file rather than rename it, then the pattern can match other names in addition to the one in which you are interested, because you can use *rm −i*. The *−i* option causes *rm* to run interactively, soliciting removal confirmation from you for each file. Respond with y (yes) for the file you want to remove and n (no) for the others as shown below:

```
% rm -i *abc*
rm: remove !abc? n
rm: remove !abc and def? y
rm: remove abc;1? n
```

Don't forget the *−i* option or *rm* will remove every file that matches the pattern.

If the filename begins with −, use *./pattern* to prevent *rm* from interpreting the leading dash as a flag.

Quoting Special Characters Yourself

If you want to quote special characters yourself, use the guidelines given below. Hard-to-use filenames usually fall into one of the following categories:

- *Filenames containing one or a few special characters*

  The names *abc;1* and *Home Work* fit into this category. You cannot refer to either of these files directly:

  ```
  % more abc;1
  abc: No such file or directory
  1: Command not found.
  % more Home Work
  Home: No such file or directory
  Work: No such file or directory
  ```

  The ; in *abc;1* acts as a command separator and the space in *Home Work* acts as an argument separator. Use backslashes to turn off the meaning of the special characters:

  ```
  % mv abc\;1 abc1
  % more abc1
  % mv Home\ Work HomeWork
  % more HomeWork
  ```

- *Filenames containing several special characters*

  If a filename has several special characters, typing backslashes in front of all of them is a pain. Single or double quotes usually achieve the same result more easily. For example, although the following command changes the name of

My Summer Vacation (Part 2) to something easier to use, the command itself is hard to type:

```
% mv My\ Summer\ Vacation\ \(Part\ 2\) my-vac-2
```

It's simpler to use quote marks:

```
% mv 'My Summer Vacation (Part 2)' my-vac-2
```

- *Filenames containing the* ! *character*

Backslash is the only way to turn off the special meaning of ! as a history reference. Quote marks won't work:

```
% mv '!abc' abc                    Fails
abc: Event not found.
% mv \!abc abc                     Succeeds
```

If a name contains ! in addition to other special characters, put a backslash in front of the ! and put quotes around the name:

```
% mv '\!abc and def' abc-def
```

- *Filenames containing control characters*

Backslash and quote marks are useless for quoting characters like CTRL–H or CTRL–U in filenames, because these characters are interpreted as soon as you type them, not after you are finished entering the command. Solve this problem by typing CTRL–V before each such character to allow it to be entered into the command line. For example, to rename *RED* CTRL-H *ADME* to *README*, type the following:

```
% mv RED CTRL-V CTRL-H ADME README
```

Filenames containing control characters are not as uncommon as you might think. If you are using a program that prompts for an output filename, but does little sanity checking on your input, such files can be created easily. Perhaps the most annoying thing about them is that it's difficult to find out just what the control characters are. *ls* by itself is no help, because it displays all unusual characters as ? when it writes to your terminal. You can get around this problem by using *ls* in a pipeline. *ls* will then write the actual characters and you can use the following commands to discover what your filenames consist of:

```
% ls | cat -tv | more
% ls | od -bc | more
```

The first command shows control characters using ^X notation. The second displays them using octal notation. If you want to see the correspondence between octal codes and ASCII characters, use the following:

```
% man ascii
```

- *Filenames that are really obstreperous*

  For some filenames, it's quite difficult to type the full name no matter what you do. To rename *<<** New Items! (READ THIS!!) **>>*, you could type the following command, but only with great effort:

  ```
  % mv '<<** New Items\! (READ THIS\!\!) **>>' NewItems
  ```

For names like the one shown above, use filename completion or patterns to refer to the file.

Passing Special Characters to Commands

So far we've focused on special characters that occur in filenames, but the shell's quoting rules can be used for any argument, whether or not it refers to a filename. Here are some other situations in which quoting is useful:

- To group multiple words into a single argument—for example, to specify multiple word subject arguments to a mailer:

  ```
  % mail -s "schedule for tomorrow" carter < sched
  ```

  or to search through files for words that occur together:

  ```
  % grep "three word phrase" *
  ```

- To pass arguments to programs such as *grep* or *sed*, which understand their own sets of special characters. The following command deletes input lines containing digits; the expression argument must be quoted because it contains brackets:

  ```
  % sed -e '/[0-9]/d' file > file.nodigits
  ```

- To pass a TAB to a command in *tcsh*. The following command looks for lines in a file that contain a TAB character; CTRL-V is used to keep *tcsh* from trying to perform filename completion when the TAB is typed:

  ```
  % grep 'CTRL-V TAB ' file
  ```

- To pass filename patterns to programs like *find* which are capable of doing their own filename pattern matching. *find* can be used as follows to locate all filenames in or under a given directory that match a pattern:

  ```
  % find dir -name pattern -print
  ```

However, any special characters in *pattern* must be quoted so that the shell passes them through to *find*:

```
% find . -name \*.c -print          Find filenames ending with .c
% find . -name '*[A-Za-z]*' -print  Find filenames containing a letter
```

- To send mail to addresses written in UUCP style, which uses paths of the following form:

  ```
  host1!...!hostn!user
  ```

  To use these addresses from the command line, you must put backslashes in front of each ! character:

  ```
  % mail anaconda\!uunet\!postmaster
  ```

- To delay the interpretation of special characters in commands that execute remotely on another machine. Special characters must be quoted to prevent them from being interpreted until the shell on the remote host receives them:

  ```
  % rsh cobra rm "~/src/*.bak"          Remove backup files from ~/src directory on cobra
  % rcp adder:/var/log/syslog\* /tmp    Copy syslog files from adder to local /tmp directory
  ```

Referring to a File When the Name Has a Leading Dash

If you create a file with a name that begins with a dash, you could have trouble using the file. Many commands consider arguments with a leading dash to be processing options and not filenames, *mv* and *rm* in particular. Files with names that begin with a dash are difficult to rename or remove:

```
% mv -myfile1 myfile1
usage: mv [-if] f1 f2 or mv [-if] f1 ... fn d1
% rm -myfile2
usage: rm [-rif] file ...
```

This problem is not exactly a quoting issue, but the dash is treated specially in this situation and you need to be able to work around it. Try using an equivalent filename that does not begin with a dash:

```
% mv ./-myfile1 myfile1
% rm ./-myfile2
```

+, when used as the first character of a filename, will cause problems to a more limited extent than −, because fewer commands take options that begin with +. Nevertheless, you should still avoid giving files names like +*abc*, because certain commonly used commands like *more* and *vi* are among those that look for + options.

Using Partial Quoting

Sometimes only part of an argument should be quoted. Suppose you want to list the contents of *~ann/Volume II*, i.e., the *Volume II* directory under *ann*'s account. You cannot leave the name unquoted because it contains a space, but you cannot quote the whole thing, either, because such quotes would prevent *~ann* from being expanded properly:

```
% ls ~ann/Volume II
/usr/staff/ann/Volume not found
II not found
% ls "~ann/Volume II"
~ann/Volume II not found
```

Instead, quote the space with a backslash or use quote marks to quote part of the name. The following commands allow expansion of *~ann* while preventing the space from acting as an argument separator:

```
% ls ~ann/Volume\ II            (or)
% ls ~ann/'Volume II'
```

Quoting Oddities

The quoting rules have a few exceptions. You probably won't run into these often, but it's good to be aware of them:

- ! or $ at the end of an argument is not interpreted as special and does not need quoting:

  ```
  % echo x! x$
  x! x$
  ```

- A backslash inside quote marks is normally left alone, as demonstrated below where the quotes protect the backslash in the second and third arguments:

  ```
  % echo \x '\x' "\x"
  x \x \x
  ```

However, if a backslash occurs before !, it is always interpreted as a quote character. Notice how the backslash disappears in the following example, even when it appears within quote marks:

```
% echo \!x '\!x' "\!x"
!x !x !x
```

This result occurs because \ is the only way to turn off !; therefore, \! is interpreted as a literal ! regardless of its context.

- !, `, and $ normally retain their special meaning inside double quotes. You can turn off ! and ` (but not $) by preceding each with a backslash:

```
% echo "\!x" "\`x\`"
!x `x`
% echo "\$shell"
/bin/tcsh
```

Inside double quotes, a $ is interpreted as beginning a variable reference, and you cannot turn it off, even with a backslash.

- A single quote cannot appear within a single-quoted string, even if you use a backslash. The same is true of double quotes within a double-quoted string:

```
% echo '\''
Unmatched '.
% echo "\""
Unmatched ".
```

12

Using Commands To Generate Arguments

This chapter describes how to use one command to supply arguments for another. This valuable technique can be used by itself or in conjunction with other argument generators, such as pattern-matching operators.

Command Substitution

The shell helps you issue commands by providing shorthand methods for specifying command arguments. The most common technique is to use filename patterns to generate a list of files, so that you don't have to type each filename explicitly. For example, to edit all the C source files in your current directory, you could select them easily with the following pattern:

```
% vi *.c
```

But filename patterns have certain limitations. You cannot use them to select filenames based on file content, to search through directory hierarchies, or to select files based on criteria such as age, ownership, size, type, etc.

For such tasks, other file selection strategies may be used. For example, it may be relatively easy to generate the appropriate filenames by running a command. Suppose you want to identify the files that contain the string "gaboon," and then edit them to say "viper" instead. A filename pattern by itself will not tell you which files contain "gaboon," but a command consisting of *grep* in conjunction with a pattern works quite well, as shown below:

```
% grep -li gaboon *
```

The command shown above generates the names of the qualifying files at your terminal. Unfortunately, the command doesn't help you to edit the files, and manually retyping the filenames produced by *grep* into an editor command is a dreary prospect, especially if many files are involved. A technique called command substitution is helpful in such cases. Command substitution allows you to run the *grep* command and then insert the output directly into another command line. To edit files containing "gaboon" using command substitution, place the *grep* command inside backquotes:

```
% vi `grep -li gaboon *`
```

The shell evaluates the backquoted *grep* command and replaces the command with its output (with newlines changed to spaces). The resulting *vi* command line is then executed. As a result, if *grep* produces the filenames *index.ms*, *intro.ms*, *preface.ms*, *reference.ms*, and *taxonomy.ms* as output, the *vi* command is equivalent to the following:

```
% vi index.ms intro.ms preface.ms reference.ms taxonomy.ms
```

Backquoted commands are often used to produce a list of filenames (as shown above), but they can be used to generate other types of output such as numbers or status reports. For example, you can put the following command in your `~/.login` file to learn how many people are on your system each time you log in:

```
echo "There are `who|wc -l` users logged in."
```

Backquoted commands can contain history or variable references:

```
% which spell
/usr/bin/spell
% file `!!`
file `which spell`
/usr/bin/spell: executable shell script
% more !$
more `which spell`

% set dir = /usr/bin
% echo "$dir contains `ls $dir|wc -l` files."
/usr/bin contains 322 files.
```

Backquoted commands are evaluated inside double quotes, but not inside single quotes:

```
% echo "Mail queue backlog: `mailq|head -1`"
Mail queue backlog: Mail Queue (176 requests)
% echo 'Mail queue backlog: `mailq|head -1`'
Mail queue backlog: `mailq|head -1`
```

You cannot put one backquoted command inside another; backquotes that appear inside other backquotes are not valid.

Finding Files

find is a useful utility for specifying filename arguments because it can search through entire directory trees. Suppose you are at the top of a multiple directory project that contains *README* files in several of its directories. (This could be a programming project, a research project containing data files from several related experiments, a *gopher* or *ftp* archive hierarchy, etc.) The *find* command can help you locate the files:

```
% find . -name README -print
```

This *find* command means "beginning at . (the current directory), look for files named *README* and print (display) their pathnames." *find* is useful with command substitution to select the *README* files for other commands. For example, to look at the files, do this:

```
% more `find . -name README -print`
```

To print them, do this:

```
% pr `find . -name README -print` | lpr
```

The commands shown above may look a little intimidating if you are not accustomed to using *find*, but consider the prospect of accomplishing the same thing by *cd*-ing into each directory of the project looking for *README* files and issuing individual *more* or *pr* commands. No thanks!

We'll use *find* in simple form several times in this chapter, but you should take a look at its manual page to get an idea of some of the other things you can do with *find*. Another valuable source of information for *find* is *UNIX Power Tools* from O'Reilly & Associates.

Taking Arguments from a File

If the filenames that you want to use are already stored in a file, you can use command substitution to insert the file's contents into a command line like this:

```
% command `cat names`
```

names can be created any way you like. One of the most basic methods for processing a set of filenames from a directory is to list the directory's contents into a file, edit the file to remove the names of no interest, and then substitute the file's contents into another command. This method is illustrated below:

```
% ls > names                    List filenames into names
% vi names                      Edit names to remove extraneous filenames
% command `cat names`           Pass remaining filenames to command
```

Processing Arguments Individually

If you want to produce filenames with a command but process them individually, use a *foreach* loop. Assume that you want to make a backup copy of each of the "gaboon" files before revising them. You could do the following:

```
% foreach f (`grep -li gaboon *`)
? cp $f $f.bak
? end
```

foreach runs the commands in the loop, one time for each argument named inside the parentheses. Each time through the loop, the variable *f* is assigned the name of the next successive argument (in this case, the next filename produced by *grep*). The prompt changes until you type the *end* line, to remind you that the loop contents are being collected. Finally, the loop is executed.

Repeating Substituted Commands

You will often perform a series of operations on the same set of files; therefore, when you use a command to generate a list of filenames, you may find it desirable to use the list more than once. Suppose you want to revise the "gaboon" files, and then individually format and print each file. You could do the following:

```
% vi `grep -li gaboon *`
% foreach f (`grep -li gaboon *`)
? groff -ms $f | lpr
? end
```

However, the method displayed above involves inefficient typing. A backquoted command counts as a single argument in a command line; therefore, you can easily repeat the command via a history operator:

```
% vi `grep -li gaboon *`
% foreach f (`!$`)                    Repeat final argument of previous command
foreach f (`grep -li gaboon *`)
? groff -ms $f | lpr
? end
```

Using your history to repeat a command substitution saves typing, but that method actually runs the substituted command again. If you think that the command may take a long time to complete, running it more than once is inefficient and a waste of time. A different kind of repetition would be preferable.

One way of running a command once, but using its output multiple times, requires that you save the output in a variable, and then refer to the variable when you need to use the list of filenames:

```
% set args = `grep -li gaboon *`
% vi $args
% foreach f ($args)
? groff -ms $f | lpr
? end
```

Another way to avoid running a time-consuming command multiple times is to save the command's output in a file, and then substitute the file's contents into other commands using *cat*. I use this technique to rummage through the Imake-files of the X Window System distribution to see how various configuration parameters are used. The X software consists of thousands of files, so running *find* in the

X hierarchy is something to be avoided whenever possible. Instead, I generate, only once, a master list *im.list* of the pathnames for all the Imakefiles:

```
% cd top-of-X-tree
% find . -name Imakefile -print > im.list
```

If I have this list in hand, I don't need to repeat the *find* command every time I want to search the Imakefiles. I can simply repeat the output by inserting the contents of the file list into other commands:

```
% grep -l CrossCompiling `cat im.list`
% grep -l Threads.tmpl `cat im.list`
% etc.
```

Deferred Command Substitution

In the most direct form of command substitution, the output of a command that generates arguments is substituted immediately into the command that uses the arguments. The strategy of saving the arguments in a file and inserting the file's contents into another command decouples argument generation from argument use, which in effect defers command substitution. This method was used in the previous section for reasons of efficiency (to avoid running a lengthy *find* command more than once), but the method is useful in other situations as well. For example, you can examine the argument list to check it, or to modify the list before passing it to another command. These techniques are discussed below.

Verifying the Argument List

You should not always put a backquoted command directly into the command that uses its output. The argument-generating command might produce unexpected output, or no output at all, as discussed below.

Dealing with unexpected output

The argument-generating command might not produce the type of output you expect. The single-character difference between the following command lines is significant:

```
% vi `grep -li gaboon *`
% vi `grep -i gaboon *`
```

The *grep* command in the first command line lists only the names of the files containing lines matching the search string. This is the desired output. The *grep* command in the second command line lists the matching lines themselves. This is not the desired output. If you inadvertently forget to add the *-l* option, the resulting command line will contain the contents of the matching lines, instead of the names of the files you want to edit.

Deferring command substitution gives you a chance to check the arguments and revise the argument-generating command before using the output:

```
% grep -i gaboon * > names          Generate the arguments
% cat names                         Check output, notice that it is incorrect
% !g:s/-i/-li                       Fix grep options and generate the arguments again
grep -li gaboon * > names
% cat names                         Check again; this time the output is correct
% vi `!!`                           Edit files
vi `cat names`
```

Dealing with missing output

The argument-generating command might not produce any output at all. If this occurs, the command that you expected to process files could end up simply waiting to read from the terminal. Consider the command to locate and print *README* files in a directory tree:

```
% pr `find . -name README -print` | lpr
```

If there are no *README* files in the tree, *find* produces no output and the command is equivalent to this:

```
% pr | lpr
```

As a result, you're waiting for the command to print some files, and the command is waiting for you to type input at the terminal.

Deferred command substitution is useful to avoid getting hung up by a command that sits and waits for input from the terminal:

```
% find . -name README -print > names     Generate argument list
% cat names                               Check the list
% pr `!!` | lpr                           If the list of names is non-empty, print files
pr `cat names` | lpr
```

If *names* was empty, you simply wouldn't bother to run the *pr* command.

Verifying arguments using tee

Argument generation and verification can be combined into a single command by using *tee*, which simultaneously displays its input on the terminal and writes it to a file. The command sequences shown above can be issued by using *tee* as follows:

```
% grep -i gaboon * | tee names
% grep -li gaboon * | tee names
% vi `cat names`

% find . -name README -print | tee names
% pr `cat names` | lpr
```

The filename argument to *tee* is an output file, rather than an input file; therefore, when you use *tee*, do not use > to save the output.

Modifying the Argument List

You cannot always use a single command to generate the list of filenames of interest to you. If necessary, produce the list in two or more steps. First save the argument list in a file, then process the file to modify the list before substituting it into another command.

Suppose that you want to find and possibly compress files in your account that are larger than 500 blocks. Use *find* to generate an initial list of candidate filenames. Then, edit the list to remove the names of any files that you wish to leave uncompressed (or that have already been compressed). Finally, compress those files that remain in the list. The command sequence might look like this:

```
% find ~ -type f -size +500 -print > names     Identify large files
% vi names                                      Edit the list of filenames
% compress `cat names`                          Compress the files in the resulting list
```

Another type of two-step process occurs when you produce a list of filenames from which you generate secondary lists for substitution into other commands. The earlier example that showed how I searched through the Imakefiles of the X distribution is an example where this technique is useful. The first step is to construct the file *im.list* containing the *Imakefile* pathnames. From this list I produce a secondary list that describes which Imakefiles contain a particular symbol:

```
% grep -l symbol `cat im.list` > names     Determine which Imakefiles contain symbol
```

Now, I can substitute the secondary list into commands:

```
% more `cat names`                         Look at the files
% pr !$ | lpr                              Print them
```

Since I've left the original list intact, I can continue to use it for other searches.

When To Avoid Command Substitution

Some circumstances make command substitution difficult to use. Such circumstances could require a little extra care; others could require a completely different method for processing your argument list.

Filenames Containing Special Characters

Do not use command substitution to generate a list of filename arguments if the names contain special characters. Filenames containing spaces or other characters with special meanings turn into multiple or malformed arguments. Suppose you want to edit files containing a particular string, using the following command:

```
% vi `grep -l string *`
```

If one of the qualifying files produced by *grep* is named *Some File*, the file ends up in the *vi* command as two arguments (*Some* and *File*), rather than one. You could avoid this problem by quoting the filenames as follows:

```
% vi `grep -l string * | sed "s/.*/'&'/"`
```

However, the command shown above is very ugly and easy to mistype. Quoting the names could be tricky if the names contain quote characters. You would benefit from a habit of naming your files without using special characters.

Using xargs Instead of Command Substitution

A command could produce a list of hundreds or thousands of filenames. For example, if you were trying to locate all the files under your current directory that contain a given string, you might try the command shown below. However, if you have a lot of files, the backquoted command might produce so much output that the command substitution would fail:

```
% grep -l string `find . -type f -print`
Too many words from ``.
```

Such a situation could occur if your system or the shell imposes a per-process limit on the size of argument lists. If you're lucky, the command will simply fail with an error message (as shown above). If you're not so lucky, you might end up with a hung shell that has to be killed from a separate login session. The limits imposed sometimes depend on how the filenames are generated, e.g., command substitution versus filename pattern expansion. This uncertainty is unfortunate in that sometimes the only way for you to determine if a command will work is to try it.

The *xargs* utility provides an alternative to command substitution when you need to process a large number of files. The arguments to *xargs* consist of the command you want to execute, except that you do not specify any filenames. The input to *xargs* consists of the names of the files to be processed. Therefore, instead of typing the following:

```
% grep -l string `find . -type f -print`
```

You could rewrite the command line to use *xargs*:

```
% find . -type f -print | xargs grep -l string
```

Since the filenames produced by *find* are presented to *xargs* as input rather than on the command line, there can be any number of them. *xargs* reads the names, splits them into smaller lists, and passes each list as arguments to a separate invocation of the command that *xargs* is to execute. This behavior keeps the size of individual argument lists reasonable.[*]

---

[*] *xargs* has options for controlling how it splits up the input arguments and passes them to the command it invokes. Consult the manual page for more information.

If you already have a list of filenames in a file, you can use *xargs* in the following manner:

```
% xargs command < names
```

To gain experience with *xargs*, use it to execute *echo*. By doing so, you can view how *xargs* divides its input into argument lists. For a simple demonstration, list the contents of any directory that has more than a few files in it and observe the result:

```
% ls /bin | xargs echo
```

xargs receives a list of filenames as input from *ls*, divides up the names into smaller lists, and then passes each list to *echo*.

Limitations of xargs

xargs doesn't work properly if the filenames contain spaces or other special characters, as with command substitution.

xargs doesn't work if the command to be executed is really an alias.

13

Navigating the File System

Your home directory is your initial location when you log in, but you'll probably work at other locations as well. You should make a practice of moving to the directory that contains the files you want to work on. This chapter discusses the capabilities that the shell provides for traveling quickly and easily through the file system:

• Basic commands for moving around the file system

• The directory stack (what it is, how it helps you, and how to use it)

• Using aliases and variables to make changing directories an easy task

As you become more adept at moving around, you may notice how easy it is to forget where you are. Chapter 14, *Keeping Track of Where You Are*, discusses how to avoid "getting lost" in the file system.

Moving Around

The primary command for changing your location in the file system is *cd* (change directory), which can move you into any directory for which you have permission. In order to use *cd* effectively, you should learn the basic idioms:

`% cd`	Move to your home directory
`% cd ..`	Move up to parent of current directory
`% cd dir1`	Move to *dir1* under current directory
`% cd dir1/dir2/dir3`	Move to directory several levels below current directory
`% cd /`	Move to root directory
`% cd /dir1`	Move to *dir1* under root directory
`% cd /dir1/dir2/dir3`	Move to directory several levels below root directory

Convenient shorthand conventions for use in changing directories are ~ (for your own home directory) and ~*name* (for the home directory of user *name*). These conventions are illustrated below:

% cd ~/Mail	Move to your own *Mail* directory
% cd ~mary	Move to home directory of *mary*'s account
% cd ~terrell/Projects	Move to *Projects* directory under *terrell*'s account

You will find that using a name like ~*mary* is much easier than using an absolute pathname like */usr/staff/admin/mary*; the former requires less typing and you don't even have to know the corresponding pathname.

Working in Multiple Locations

Your work probably involves accessing information that's stored in more than one directory. For example, suppose you're working in directory A, and then change into directory B, to check something briefly before continuing your work in directory A. In other situations, you might move back and forth between directories on a more extended basis. Suppose you're working in ~*/src/myprog* to modify the source code for a program *myprog*, but occasionally need to review the contents of some of the system header files in */usr/include*. One method of moving between directories is to supply a pathname each time you change directory:

```
% cd /usr/include
% cd ~/src/myprog
% cd /usr/include
% cd ~/src/myprog
% etc.
```

However, the method shown above is inefficient and tedious. You could visit and revisit a set of locations more easily if you could type a directory's name the first time you move into it, and then return to it later without having to type the name again. The following sections describe the shell's facilities for changing directories in this manner.

Using cd – To Return to the Previous Directory

In *tcsh*, the command *cd* – returns to your previous location, so successive *cd* – commands provide a convenient way to alternate between two directories. If you are currently in ~*/src/myprog*, you can alternate with */usr/include* as shown below:

% cd /usr/include	Move to */usr/include*
% cd -	Return to ~*/src/myprog*
% cd -	Return to */usr/include*
% cd -	Return to ~*/src/myprog*
% etc.	

However, the – mechanism remembers only one directory. If while in */usr/include* you type *cd sys* to move into */usr/include/sys, tcsh* forgets that you were once in ~*/src/myprog*. That means you cannot use *cd* – to return to it. To ensure that you can return to ˜/*src/myprog* easily, no matter where else you move, you must save ˜/*src/myprog* on the directory stack.

Using the Directory Stack

cd has two cousins, *pushd* (push directory) and *popd* (pop directory), which can change your location in the file system. These commands also allow you to remember directories and return to them later. They do their work using the shell's directory stack, which contains the current directory and any others that you wish to remember. Unlike *cd −* (which is available only in *tcsh*), the stack manipulation commands are available in both *csh* and *tcsh*.[*]

pushd adds entries to the stack and *popd* removes them. Both commands show the stack contents after changing directory. If you forget which directories are on the stack, *dirs* displays the stack without changing directory. The common forms of *pushd* and *popd* are shown in Table 13–1.

Using the directory stack is like placing markers in a book so that you can return to specific locations simply by turning to the appropriate bookmark. You type a directory's name explicitly only the first time you move into it, then return to it later using a notation that is quicker and easier than typing out the name again.

Table 13–1: Directory Stack Commands

Command	Description
pushd `dir`	Add `dir` to stack and change to it
pushd	Exchange top two stack entries
pushd +`n`	Rotate stack so entry `n` is on top
popd	Drop top entry and return to previous entry
popd +`n`	Drop entry `n` entry from stack (*tcsh*, some versions of *csh*)
dirs	Display current stack contents

Reconsider the scenario of switching between ˜/*src/myprog* and /*usr/include*, with regard to the stack-manipulating commands. Your current directory is always on top of the stack, which therefore always has at least one entry. At login time, the top entry is your home directory. When you move into ˜/*src/myprog* with *cd*, the top entry changes to reflect your new location:

```
% dirs                              Directory stack at login time
~
% cd ~/src/myprog ; dirs            Move into ~/src/myprog, then show stack
~/src/myprog
```

---

[*] Actually, that isn't quite true. Some versions of *csh* do not implement the directory stack. If you are stuck with one of those, consider switching to *tcsh*, because access to the stack mechanism is important for effective shell use.

pushd with a directory argument changes into that directory and pushes it onto the stack. Using *pushd* is similar to using *cd*, except that your previous location remains on the stack, under the new entry:

```
% pushd /usr/include
/usr/include ~/src/myprog
```

pushd displays the modified stack so that you can see the stack contents, with your current directory leftmost.

After you have two directories on the stack, *pushd* with no argument exchanges them. This gives you an easy way to bounce between two locations without constantly typing directory names:

```
% pushd                              Return to ~/src/myprog
~/src/myprog /usr/include
% pushd                              Return to /usr/include
/usr/include ~/src/myprog
```

When you are done working in a directory, *popd* removes the top entry from the stack, returns you to the directory specified by the previous entry, and displays the new stack contents:

```
% popd                               Pop /usr/include, return to ~/src/myprog
~/src/myprog
```

In *tcsh*, *pushd* understands – to mean your previous location, just as *cd* does. Consequently, if you pop the current directory with *popd*, then decide you still want it, *pushd* – returns the directory to the stack:

```
% pushd -                            Put /usr/include back on the stack and move there
/usr/include ~/src/myprog
```

Additional *pushd dir* commands put more entries on the stack:

```
% pushd /usr/local/lib
/usr/local/lib /usr/include ~/src/myprog
% pushd ~/Mail
~/Mail /usr/local/lib /usr/include ~/src/myprog
```

However, when the stack has more than two entries, you need a more general way of referring to each directory (*pushd* with no argument accesses only the top two entries and is, as a result, insufficient). Stack entries are numbered beginning with 0, and you refer to them using +*n* notation. For example, to change into */usr/include* using the stack from the above example, start from 0 and count from the left to see that */usr/include* is entry two. Then switch to that entry as shown below:

```
% pushd +2
/usr/include ~/src/myprog ~/Mail /usr/local/lib
```

Look closely at what happens to the stack: *pushd +2* rotates the stack to put entry two on top. Because entries are numbered from zero and not one, entry two is the third entry and *pushd +2* rotates the stack three times, instead of two. Keep this subtle point in mind, or you'll always be off by one entry.

In *tcsh* and some versions of *csh*, you can use *popd +n* to remove entry *n* without changing your current location:

```
% popd +3                          Remove /usr/local/lib from stack
/usr/include ~/src/myprog ~/Mail
```

To clear the entire stack, use *dirs −c* (*tcsh* only).

Stack Display Formats

In *csh*, stack entries are normally displayed as full pathnames, except that directories under your home directory are displayed using ~ notation. *tcsh* provides a fuller notation, using *~name* to display directories under the accounts for other users.

csh allows you to use *dirs −l* to display the stack entries using long names (i.e., with ~ notation expanded to full pathnames). This option also happens to be the only one that *csh* provides for varying the stack display; therefore, the rest of this section applies only to *tcsh*.

tcsh provides other display options in addition to *−l* and allows you to apply them to other commands. The examples shown below use *dirs. cd*, *pushd*, and *popd* also accept the flags shown.

Suppose that the stack looks like this:

```
% dirs
/usr/include ~/Mail ~ftp/pub ~
```

As with *csh*, *dirs −l* causes long names to be used:

```
% dirs -l
/usr/include /usr/staff/dubois/Mail /usr/ftp/pub /usr/staff/dubois
```

dirs −n formats the display so that if an entry would extend past the end of the screen and wrap around, that entry is instead printed in its entirety on the next line. This formatting style can make the display easier to read.

dirs −v produces "vertical" output, i.e., with each entry on its own line. In addition, entry numbers are displayed:

```
% dirs -v
0    /usr/include
1    ~/Mail
2    ~ftp/pub
3    ~
```

dirs −v is helpful when you want to refer to entries using *+n* (for *pushd* or *popd*) or *=n* (in command-line arguments), because you can see the entry numbers without having to count them out. You can use multiple flags, e.g., *dirs –lv* prints vertical output using long names.

pushd and *popd* normally print the stack. If you do not want this feedback, set the *pushdsilent* shell variable in your ˜/.cshrc file:

```
set pushdsilent
```

To tell *pushd* or *popd* to print the stack even when the *pushdsilent* variable has been set, use *–p* (or *–l*, *–n*, or *–v* if you want one of the alternate stack display formats).

Referring to Stack Entries in Command Arguments

tcsh allows you to begin command arguments with *=n* or with *=–*, to refer to stack entry *n* or to the final entry. This notation makes it easy to access directories named on your stack without actually moving into them. Suppose you are in ˜/*src/myprog* and your stack looks like this:

```
% dirs -v
0    ˜/src/myprog
1    /usr/include
2    ˜/Mail
```

If you want to take a look at */usr/include/syslog.h*, you could switch into */usr/include*, run *more syslog.h*, then switch back to ˜/*src/myprog*. But you'll do less work if you stay where you are and look at the file with a single command:

```
% more =1/syslog.h
```

tcsh expands =1 to stack entry 1 (*/usr/include*). To find files in ˜/*Mail* that contain messages pertaining to *myprog*, you could use either of these commands:

```
% grep myprog =2/*
% grep myprog =-/*
```

Filename completion works for arguments that begin with *=n*:

```
% more =1/lo█                        Type prefix, then hit TAB
% more =1/locale.h█                  tcsh completes the name
```

=n notation is so convenient that you may find yourself putting directories on the stack, even if you do not intend to change into them often. By placing a directory on the stack, you can refer to its files using *=n* rather than typing directory pathnames.

An Alternative to the Directory Stack

If you are using a window system, you can pop up multiple windows and move into a different directory in each window. Then, by switching windows, you can switch between directories without using the stack.

You will probably want to choose whichever technique is most appropriate for the circumstances. If you simply need to switch into another directory to run a short command or two, you would most likely use the stack. On the other hand, if you need to refer to the contents of a file repeatedly as you run other commands, you would do better to keep the file open in a separate window.

Letting the Shell Find Directories for You

The directory stack makes it easier to revisit a directory after you have been there, but you still have to type the directory's name the first time you enter it. The shell can make that easier to do, by reducing the need to type multiple component pathnames to get to the directories you want. The shell accomplishes this feat by allowing you to set up a directory search path, a mechanism analogous to the command search path.

When you run a command, you usually type only the command's basename (the last component of its full pathname). The shell finds the command by looking in the directories named in your *path* variable. In similar fashion, if you set the *cdpath* shell variable, the shell understands its value to be a list of locations in which to look when you give a directory argument to *cd* or *pushd*. In other words, if you enter *cd dir* or *pushd dir* and the shell doesn't find *dir* in your current directory, it will search the directories named in *cdpath*.[*]

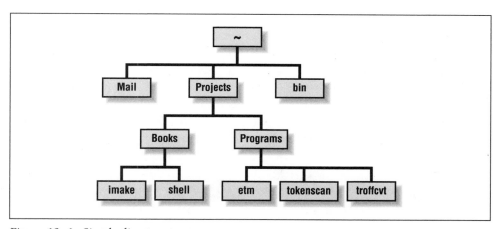

Figure 13–1: Simple directory tree

Suppose the directory layout for your account is as shown in Figure 13–1, and you want to successively change into the *Programs, Shell, Mail,* and *tokenscan*

---

[*] The shell ignores *cdpath* for pathnames that begin with /, ./, or ../ since by beginning a name that way you explicitly "anchor" it to the root directory, your current directory, or the parent of your current directory. This allows you to defeat the search mechanism if you want.

directories. If you didn't set *cdpath*, you would have to type out pathnames as follows:

```
% cd ~/Projects/Programs
% cd ~/Projects/Books/Shell
% cd ~/Mail
% cd ~/Projects/Programs/tokenscan
```

Much of that typing can be eliminated by setting *cdpath*. For example, to tell the shell to search for directories in your home directory and in the *Projects, Books,* and *Programs* directories, set *cdpath* in your `~/.cshrc` file as follows:

```
set cdpath = ( ~ ~/Projects ~/Projects/{Books,Programs} )
```

Now, you can change into your directories by typing only their basenames:

```
% cd Programs
% cd Shell
% cd Mail
% cd tokenscan
```

The directory tree shown in Figure 13–1 is relatively simple; therefore, if you set *cdpath* to a list of a few key locations, you can then change into any of the directories by using the basenames. If your account layout is more extensive, you will not always have this capability. However, by picking only those directories under which you tend to focus your current activities, you should be able to eliminate much or even most of your pathname typing.[*]

The directories named by *cdpath* can be located anywhere, not only in your own account. For example, a system administrator might often change into the subdirectories of */usr/spool* using commands like these:

```
% cd /usr/spool/lpd
% pushd /usr/spool/mqueue
```

If so, */usr/spool* would be a good addition to *cdpath*, because the commands shown above would become simpler:

```
% cd lpd
% pushd mqueue
```

One directory that you don't have to include in *cdpath* is your current directory (`.`), since *cd* and *pushd* look there first, anyway.

Limitations of cdpath

The *cdpath* mechanism has some limitations you should be aware of:

---

[*] This implies that as your activities change, you may want to adjust your *cdpath* from time to time.

- *cdpath* works bèst when your directories have distinctive names. If two of the directories in your *cdpath* have subdirectories named *xyz*, you will have a harder time changing into the second one. (*cd xyz* will move you to the second directory only if you are already located in its parent. Otherwise, you need to type an explicit path to that directory.)

- *cdpath* applies only to *cd* or *pushd*. As a result, although *cd tokenscan* takes you to the *tokenscan* directory regardless of your location, *ls tokenscan* doesn't work unless *tokenscan* is in your current directory.

- Filename completion doesn't know about *cdpath*, either. Typing `ls tok` and hitting the completion key doesn't work unless *tokenscan* is in your current directory.

- Some versions of *csh* fail to use *cdpath* properly if a plain file exists in your current directory and has the same name as the directory you want to change into. For example, *cd xyz* fails if a file named *xyz* exists in your current directory, even if an *xyz* directory exists in one of your *cdpath* directories:

```
% cd xyz
xyz: Not a directory
```

If you see the error message shown above, and you are sure that there is a directory in your *cdpath* containing an *xyz* directory, suspect this bug. *tcsh* doesn't have this problem.

Using Aliases and Variables To Move Around

This section discusses how to use aliases to help you issue directory-changing commands more easily, and how to use variables to provide arguments for those commands.

Moving Around Using Aliases

One simple way to ease file system navigation is to create shorter command names using aliases:

```
alias pu pushd
alias po popd
```

Certain idiomatic forms of *cd* are also easily turned into aliases. Those shown below allow you to type `..`, `/`, or `-` to change into your parent directory, the root directory, or your previous directory:

```
alias .. cd ..
alias / cd /
alias - cd -                    (This one works only for tcsh)
```

If you visit certain locations frequently, aliases can make them easier to get to. A system administrator who often works in the mail queue directory or in */usr/adm* might find these aliases useful:

```
alias mq cd /usr/spool/mqueue
alias adm cd /usr/adm
```

A programmer, on the other hand, would be more likely to use aliases like these:

```
alias ui cd /usr/include
alias uis cd /usr/include/sys
alias ul cd /usr/lib
```

Moving Around Using Variables

Commonly used directories can be accessed using variables rather than aliases. For example, to give yourself an alternate way of getting into */usr/include*, set a variable in your `~/.cshrc` file, like this:

```
set ui = /usr/include
```

Then refer to the variable in directory-changing commands:

```
% cd $ui
% pushd $ui
```

Changing directory using an alias usually requires less typing than changing using variables, because you are typing one word (*ui*), instead of two (*cd $ui*). However, the alias can be used in only one manner (to move you to a given directory). A variable that refers to a directory can be used in many other ways. For example, you can access the directory's contents, regardless of your location:

```
% ls $ui/sys              List files in /usr/include/sys
% more $ui/stdio.h        Look at /usr/include/stdio.h
% grep NFILE $ui/*.h      Search files in /usr/include for NFILE
```

In *tcsh*, variables that specify pathnames can also be used with filename completion:

```
% more $ui/me█            Type prefix, then hit TAB
% more $ui/memory.h█      tcsh completes the name
```

Combining Aliases and Variables

Aliases and variables provide somewhat different conveniences. In order to benefit from both, use them together. Suppose you are managing a Usenet installation and have duties that involve frequent use of the following directories:

```
/usr/lib/news              News library directory
/usr/log/news              News logging directory
/usr/spool/news            News spool directory
/usr/spool/news/out.going  News outgoing spool directory
```

To help you move among these directories and access their files, you can put the variable and alias definitions shown below in your *˜/.cshrc* file:

```
set nlib = /usr/lib/news
set nlog = /usr/log/news
set nspool = /usr/spool/news
set nout = $nspool/out.going
alias nlib cd $nlib
alias nlog cd $nlog
alias nspool cd $nspool
alias nout cd $nout
```

The aliases let you move around quickly to any of the four main directories. The variables let you easily access the files and subdirectories, even if you don't happen to be in the particular directory of interest:

`% emacs $nlib/newsfeeds`	Edit */usr/lib/news/newsfeeds*
`% ls $nspool/junk	wc -1`	Count articles in */usr/spool/news/junk*
`% tail -f $nlog/news.notice`	Watch */usr/log/news/news.notice*
`% du $nout`	Check size of backlog in */usr/spool/news/out.going*

This same technique can be applied to any task involving frequent use of a specific set of directories, such as software development in a multiple directory project, managing an FTP archive, or running a mailing list.

14

Keeping Track of Where You Are

When you're actively working in a directory, you can usually remember your current location. However:

- It's easy to forget where you are when you're interrupted by a phone call, take a coffee break, or pause to discuss a project with a coworker.

- When you work in a multiple-window environment that allows you to maintain several simultaneous shell sessions, it can be difficult to remember which directory window is current.

- If you have accounts on multiple systems, remembering your location becomes more complicated because you must also consider the machine you're logged in on.

One way to determine your location is to use the command line. *pwd* ("print working directory") shows the name of your current directory, *dirs* prints the directory stack, and, on most machines, either *hostname*, *uname −n*, or *who am i* will show the name of the machine you're logged into. However, there are better ways to get feedback on your location. This chapter discusses how to set up your `˜/.cshrc` file to have the shell provide that information automatically, so you don't have to waste time running commands to figure out where you are.

Types of Location Reporting

One method of getting location information is to have the shell announce directory changes when you use *cd*, *pushd*, or *popd*. *pushd* and *popd* print the directory stack automatically. To have *cd* do the same, alias it to your ˜/.*cshrc* file, like this:

```
alias cd 'cd \!*;dirs'
```

An alternative strategy arranges for continuous location reporting. This strategy lets you determine your location instantly, whether or not you change your directory. Continuous reporting is particularly valuable in a multiple-session environment that involves a lot of switching between windows.

To have the shell produce a continuous display of your location, first decide where you want to have the information displayed. Your prompt is a good location. Another likely place, if you use a window system, is the titlebar of your terminal windows. Commands to produce each type of display are discussed in the following sections.

Because the point of displaying the current location is to keep you informed as you work at the command line, the commands in ˜/.*cshrc* that set up the display need to be executed only for interactive shells. You should place those commands inside the following construct, which determines whether or not the shell is interactive by examining the *prompt* shell variable:

```
if ($?prompt) then
    commands to set up location display
endif
```

prompt is given a default value only by interactive shells. Therefore, non-interactive shells (e.g., those started to run scripts, or to run shell escapes from within an editor or mailer) skip the commands inside the *if*-statement.

As you try the commands shown in this chapter, play close attention to the quote characters used in the examples. Some examples use as many as three kinds of quotes, and won't work unless you type them exactly as shown.

Displaying Your Location in the Prompt

csh and *tcsh* differ in the facilities they provide for putting information in your prompt. First, I'll show commands that work for either shell, but are intended primarily for *csh* users. Second, I'll discuss *tcsh*'s special formatting facilities for the prompt string. For both shells, I'll show some typical prompt settings. You can, of course, experiment to find a setting that better suits your preferences.

Using csh To Display Your Location

To add the hostname to your prompt, set the *prompt* variable in your ˜/.*cshrc* file as follows:

```
set prompt = "`hostname`% "
```

If a command other than *hostname* displays the machine name on your system, make the appropriate substitution.

To include the current directory name in your prompt, create a *setprompt* alias that sets the prompt using the current location. (*setprompt* uses the *cwd* variable, which always holds the pathname of your current working directory.) Then, alias the directory-changing commands (*cd*, *pushd*, *popd*) so that they invoke *setprompt*. Add the following commands to your `~/.cshrc` file so that your prompt will be a % character preceded by the pathname of your current directory:

```
alias setprompt 'set prompt = "$cwd% "'
setprompt
alias cd 'cd \!*;setprompt'
alias pushd 'pushd \!*;setprompt'
alias popd 'popd \!*;setprompt'
```

Note that *setprompt* is executed after it is defined. This is necessary to set the prompt to the proper initial value. Otherwise, the prompt would not be set until you changed directory for the first time.

If you prefer to display only the tail (last component) of the current directory's pathname, change $cwd to $cwd:t in the definition of *setprompt*:

```
alias setprompt 'set prompt = "$cwd:t% "'
```

If you want both the hostname and the current directory displayed in your prompt, change the definition of *setprompt* to one of those shown below. Each definition displays the host name and a directory name, but the first definition displays the full pathname, whereas the second definition displays only the last component:

```
alias setprompt 'set prompt = "`hostname`:$cwd% "'
alias setprompt 'set prompt = "`hostname`:$cwd:t% "'
```

For the first definition, your prompt might look like the following example as you move around:

```
viper:/usr/staff/dubois% cd /usr/spool/mqueue
viper:/usr/spool/mqueue% cd ~/Projects/Programs/tokenscan
viper:/usr/staff/dubois/Projects/Programs/tokenscan%
```

The second definition produces a different prompt, like this:

```
viper:dubois% cd /usr/spool/mqueue
viper:mqueue% cd ~/Projects/Programs/tokenscan
viper:tokenscan%
```

Using a multiple-line prompt

If you are displaying a lot of location information in your prompt, such as the full pathname of your current directory, the prompt string can become so long that you have little room left to type on the current line. Or, you may find it distracting to have the prompt change its length whenever you change directory. One solution to such problems is to display location information on a line separate from the % character by embedding a newline character in the definition of *set-prompt*. For example, if your *setprompt* alias looks like this:

```
alias setprompt 'set prompt = "$cwd% "'
```

then change it to this:

```
alias setprompt 'set prompt = "-- $cwd --\\
% "'
```

After you complete the modification given above, your prompt will look like this:

```
-- /usr/staff/dubois --
% cd /usr/spool/mqueue
-- /usr/spool/mqueue --
% cd ~/Projects/Programs/tokenscan
-- /usr/staff/dubois/Projects/Programs/tokenscan --
%
```

Breaking the prompt into multiple lines gives you ample room to display information and gives you the entire terminal width for typing commands. The format also helps you to find the % character by keeping it at a constant distance from the edge of the screen, even when the directory name varies in length.

Note that I surrounded the directory name with dashes in the multiple-line prompt. You can use other characters, but you should always use something visually distinct so that the pathname line stands out from any output produced by the previous command.

Using tcsh To Display Your Location

If you use *tcsh*, you have access to special *prompt* variable formatting sequences expressly intended for putting location information in the prompt string. Consequently, although the commands shown in the previous section do work for *tcsh*, you can achieve the same goal without messing around with a bunch of aliases.

Some useful sequences for displaying the directory or machine name are:

%/   The full pathname of the current directory.

%~   The current directory, using ~ or ~*name* abbreviations for the first part of the path (if possible). %~ usually results in shorter prompts than %/.

%c   The last component of the current directory (everything after the last slash in the full pathname).

%c*n* The last *n* components of the current directory, e.g., %c2 for the last 2 components. %c*n* abbreviates pathnames in a manner similar to that of %~.

%c0*n*
      Like %c*n*, except that when the prompt is printed and the directory pathname has more than *n* components, the number of skipped components is

indicated by a special prefix. For example, /3 indicates 3 skipped components. Alternatively, if you want skipped components to be indicated by a leading ellipsis (. . .), set the *ellipsis* shell variable in your `~/.cshrc` file as follows:

```
set ellipsis
```

%C, %Cn, %C0n

Like %c, %cn, and %c0n, but without the use of ~ pathname abbreviation.

%m, %M

The first component of the machine, or the full name. For a name like *xyz.corp.com*, %m is *xyz* and %M is *xyz.corp.com*.

%%

A % character. % followed by a non-special character (like a space) also produces a %.

For example, to set your prompt so that it displays the current directory using ~ notation, you need add only the following command to your `~/.cshrc` file:

```
set prompt = "%~% "
```

To set your prompt to *host:dir*%, where *host* is the first component of the hostname and *dir* is the current directory, use the following command:

```
set prompt = "%m:%~% "
```

If you want a multiple-line prompt, embed a newline in the prompt string. The previous *set prompt* command can be rewritten as follows:

```
set prompt = "-- %m:%~ --\
% "
```

Display Your Location in the Window Title

If you use a window system, you can also display location information in the title-bar of your terminal windows. The following discussion explains how to do so for *xterm* (the X Window System terminal program) and gives some hints for adapting the *xterm* instructions to other programs.

Several short startup file command sequences are used in this section. If you don't want to type them, you can retrieve them from the archive mentioned in Appendix C, *Other Sources of Information*. The archive also contains titlebar changing commands for programs other than those discussed here, as well as documentation for the *xterm* control sequences mentioned below.

Communicating with xterm

You can specify a window title as a command line argument when *xterm* starts up, or as a resource value in `~/.Xdefaults`, but neither method is satisfactory for changing the title on an ongoing basis as you move around the file system. However, *xterm* also understands certain control sequences, one of which sets the window title. This sequence can be sent to *xterm* at any time using *echo*, and the title can then be changed on demand. For BSD UNIX systems, the *echo* command to set the window titlebar to `title` is as follows:

```
echo -n "ESC ]2;title CTRL-G "
```

For versions of UNIX based on System V, the command is slightly different:

```
echo "ESC ]2;title CTRL-G \c"
```

Both commands suppress the newline that *echo* normally prints. (A newline is not part of the control sequence; unless you suppress it, *xterm* lets the newline pass through to your window, and you get an unwanted blank line.) The *echo* commands differ only in that BSD *echo* uses the *-n* flag to suppress the newline, whereas the System V *echo* uses \c instead. You'll need to choose the command that is appropriate for your system. If you don't know which command to use, try the first and then, if you see -n in your window every time the titlebar changes, switch to the second command. The examples shown below use the BSD version; make the appropriate substitution as necessary.

Setting the Window Title in xterm

To set up the shell to report your location in the titlebar, arrange to send *xterm* a title-change sequence whenever a directory change occurs. You can do so by aliasing *cd*, *pushd*, and *popd* in the same way that we set up the prompt-changing commands for *csh* earlier in the chapter.

Create a file in your home directory named *.settitle* that contains the commands shown below:

```
alias settitle 'echo -n "ESC ]2;$cwd CTRL-G "'
settitle
alias cd 'cd \!*;settitle'
alias pushd 'pushd \!*;settitle'
alias popd 'popd \!*;settitle'
```

To type literal ESC and CTRL-G characters into the file using your editor, you may need to precede them with CTRL-V.

You can vary the *settitle* alias definition if you like. To display only the last component of your directory in the title, change the $cwd to $cwd:t in the *echo* command, as shown below:

```
alias settitle 'echo -n "ESC ]2;$cwd:t CTRL-G "'
```

Alternatively, you could display the directory stack. Being able to see the entire stack at a glance is helpful for using *pushd +n* and for using *=n* notation to refer to stack entries in command arguments. To display the directory stack, use the following command:

```
alias settitle 'echo -n "ESC]2;`dirs`CTRL-G"'
```

After you create *.settitle*, add the following line to your ⁓/.cshrc file:

```
if (xterm =~ $TERM) source ~/.settitle
```

xterm sets the *TERM* environment variable to **xterm**, which allows the shell to tell whether or not it is running in an *xterm* window. If an *xterm* window is active the commands in *.settitle* are executed; otherwise, the commands are skipped (e.g., if you are using an ASCII terminal or are logging in through a modem from your microcomputer at home).

Setting the Window Title in Other Terminal Programs

If you are using a terminal program similar to *xterm*, you may be able to set the window title by using a slightly modified version of the method outlined in the previous section. Some examples are discussed below. If the program you use to provide terminal windows is not covered, the principles may still be similar, although the details will vary. Consult your local documentation for more specific information.

HP-UX hpterm

The HP-UX terminal program *hpterm* uses a different sequence than *xterm* to set the window title. Unfortunately, part of that sequence is the length of the title string. *tcsh* has string length operators, but *csh* does not; additionally, you can more easily generate the sequence using the following short *perl* script:

```
#!/usr/local/bin/perl
printf "\e&f0k%dD%s", length ($ARGV[0]), $ARGV[0] unless $#ARGV < 0;
```

If you name the script *hptitle*, you can use *hptitle* **string** in the *settitle* alias to set an *hpterm* window title.[*] Create a file called *.settitle-hp* in your home directory, that looks like this:

```
alias settitle 'hptitle "$cwd"'
settitle
alias cd 'cd \!*;settitle'
alias pushd 'pushd \!*;settitle'
alias popd 'popd \!*;settitle'
```

---

[*] Install the *perl* script in a directory that's listed in your *path* variable, such as ⁓/bin. You might need to change the first line of the script to reflect the location of *perl* on your system. The archive mentioned in Appendix C, *Other Sources of Information*, has a short C program that is equivalent and faster, if you're up to compiling it.

Then, put the following line in ˜/.cshrc to process .settitle-hp when you start up an
hpterm window:

```
if (hpterm =~ $TERM) source ~/.settitle-hp
```

If you use both *xterm* and *hpterm*, you can use a more extensive test to process
the file that is appropriate for the window type:

```
if (xterm =~ $TERM) then
    source ~/.settitle
else if (hpterm =~ $TERM) then
    source ~/.settitle-hp
endif
```

NCSA Telnet for Macintosh

The *xterm* control sequence for setting the titlebar works with NCSA Telnet 2.6 for
Macintosh if you select "Xterm sequences" in your terminal preferences dialog.*
Unfortunately, NCSA Telnet does not set *TERM*, so you cannot test that variable to
determine whether to execute .settitle automatically. To work around this problem,
put an *ncsa* alias in your ˜/.cshrc file, in addition to the *TERM* test:

```
if (xterm =~ $TERM) source ~/.settitle
alias ncsa source ~/.settitle
```

If you are using NCSA Telnet, then you can tell the shell to execute .settitle by typing *ncsa* after logging in.

Putting It All Together

The following is a complete example for ˜/.cshrc that puts location information in
your window titlebar when you run *xterm* or *hpterm*, and in your prompt otherwise:

```
if ($?prompt) then                          # verify that shell is interactive
    if (xterm =~ $TERM) then                # xterm is running
        source ~/.settitle
    else if (hpterm =~ $TERM) then          # hpterm is running
        source ~/.settitle-hp
    else                                    # xterm/hpterm are not running
        if ($?tcsh) then                    # shell is tcsh
            set prompt = "%~% "
        else                                # shell is csh
            alias setprompt 'set prompt = "$cwd:t% "'
            setprompt
            alias cd 'cd \!*;setprompt'
            alias pushd 'pushd \!*;setprompt'
            alias popd 'popd \!*;setprompt'
```

---

* You get to this dialog by selecting Preferences/Terminals from the Edit menu.

```
            endif
        alias ncsa source ~/.settitle
    endif
endif
```

The outermost *if*-test ensures that only interactive shells process the inner commands. Those inner commands determine whether or not *xterm* or *hpterm* are running, and take action accordingly:

- If *xterm* or *hpterm* are running, *.settitle* or *.settitle-hp* are executed to set up location display in the window title.

- If neither *xterm* nor *hpterm* are running, location information is displayed in the prompt. This is done using *tcsh*'s prompt formatting sequences if the shell is *tcsh*, and with the prompt setting aliases otherwise. Also, the *ncsa* alias is defined in case you are connecting with NCSA Telnet, so that you can display location information in the window title by typing *ncsa* after logging in.

Displaying Other Types of Information

Your prompt or window title can be used to display other kinds of information, such as your username. You can also set the text of an *xterm* window's icon so that useful information is displayed even when the window is iconified. This section discusses some of the possibilities.

Displaying the Username

If you have multiple accounts under different logins, you may find it useful to display the current username in your prompt or window title.

To display your name in the prompt with *tcsh*, just include %n in your *prompt* variable setting. The following example produces a prompt of *name@host:dir*%:

```
set prompt = "%n@%m:%~% "
```

To display the name in the prompt with *csh*, modify your *setprompt* alias to reference the appropriate environment variable (probably *USER* or *LOGNAME*, depending on what kind of system you have; we will use *USER* here). For example, to display the username and the last component of the directory name, use a definition of *setprompt* that looks like this:

```
alias setprompt 'set prompt = "${USER} $cwd:t% "'
```

To put the username in the window title, modify the *settitle* alias in your *.settitle* file. The following definition displays *name@host* followed by the directory stack:

```
alias settitle 'echo -n "ESC]2;${USER}@`hostname` `dirs`CTRL-G"'
```

In *tcsh*, the hostname is available in the *HOST* environment variable. Referencing a variable is more efficient than running *hostname*, so the alias can be rewritten as follows:

```
alias settitle 'echo -n "ESC]2;${USER}@${HOST} `dirs` CTRL-G"'
```

Setting the Window Icon in xterm

The *xterm* control sequence to change a window's icon text is similar to the one that sets the titlebar, as shown:

```
echo -n "ESC]1;string CTRL-G"
```

Putting the *echo* command in an alias lets you set the icon text easily. The following *seticon* alias sets the icon to *name@host*:

```
alias seticon 'echo -n "ESC]1;${USER}@`hostname` CTRL-G"'
```

If you use *tcsh*, use the following *seticon* alias:

```
alias seticon 'echo -n "ESC]1;${USER}@${HOST} CTRL-G"'
```

If you want *seticon* to take an argument so that you can specify the title yourself, write the *seticon* alias, as shown:

```
alias seticon 'echo -n "ESC]1;\!* CTRL-G"'
```

15

Job Control

Each command you issue starts what the shell calls a job. The shell keeps track of all jobs that have not terminated and provides facilities to manipulate those jobs. As a result, you have a lot of control over the execution of your commands. Job control has many uses:

- You can stop a job to suspend it, then resume the job at a later time. If you are composing a mail message and find that you need to check some files before proceeding, you can suspend the mailer, run a bunch of commands, and then resume the mailer where you left off. If you are using *gopher* and you see an announcement about an interesting mailing list, you don't have to quit *gopher* to sign up; instead, you can suspend *gopher*, send a mail message to join the list, and then resume *gopher* where you left off.

- Some programs provide an escape mechanism for passing single commands to a subshell for execution. Job control provides a more convenient alternative when you want to run several commands in a row. It's easier to stop the editor and restart it later than to type the escape prefix multiple times. The former method is faster because you are not starting up a separate subshell to handle each command. Additionally, you get to use filename completion and the history of your login shell, facilities which are unavailable to commands that run as shell escapes.

- You can move a job between the foreground and the background. For example, if a command takes longer than you expected, you can put it into the background and do other things while it runs. Or, you can background an *ftp* job after beginning a file transfer, work on something else in the meantime, and then return the job to the foreground when the transfer is done.

- You can kill a job, e.g., if you are trying to *rlogin* to a machine which takes so long to respond that you tire of waiting.

- You can force background jobs to stop when they try to write to your terminal, and then bring them to the foreground when you want to see their output. In this manner, you can keep the output of separate commands from getting intermixed on the screen.

This chapter discusses job states, how to obtain information about your current jobs, and how to manage job execution so that you can switch from one job to another.

Job States

You start a job by issuing a command. A job can be in one of three states: foreground, background, or stopped (suspended).* Normally, a command runs as a foreground job:

    `% grep include *.[ch]`   Run a job in the foreground

If you end a command line with &, the shell starts a background job and prints the job number and process ID:

    `% tar xf archive.tar &`   Run a job in the background
    `[1] 27163`   Shell reports the job number and process ID

If you type CTRL-Z† while a foreground job is running, the job ceases executing and becomes suspended:

    `% sort mydata > mydata2`   Start a foreground job
    CTRL-Z   Suspend it
    Stopped   Shell reports that the job has been stopped

Only one foreground job can exist at a time, but you can have multiple jobs stopped or running in the background.

If you find that you cannot stop jobs, you can consider two courses of action. First, ensure that you have the **susp** character defined:

    `% stty susp ^z`

Second, some systems require that you explicitly specify the "new" terminal driver if job control is to work:

    `% stty new`

Try the commands shown above from the command line. If either enables job control, add it to your *˜/.login* file. Otherwise, it may be that your system simply doesn't support job control. Consult with your system administrator.

---

* The terms "stopped" and "suspended" are interchangeable; both signify a non-running job.
† Or whatever your **susp** character is. If you don't know what it is, see Chapter 5, *Setting Up Your Terminal.*

Obtaining Job Information

The *jobs* command reports any jobs that you have running in the background and any jobs that are stopped. Figure 15–1 shows a job list that might result during a session of analyzing a set of data files.

```
% jobs
  [1]  -  Stopped      vi Notes.exptB
  [2]     Running      sort rawdata.[1-4] -o rawdata.1-4
  [3]     Done         grep Male rawdata3 | cut -f1,3,4 |
          Running      anova Height Weight Score > Results3
  [4]  +  Stopped      vi Results2
  [5]     Running      pr Results2 | lpr
```

```
   job number  |  job status              command line associated with job
          indicators for
        current job (+) and
          previous job (-)
```

Figure 15–1: Sample output from jobs command

If a job consists of a multiple-command pipeline, commands in the pipeline that have finished are displayed on a different line than those that are still running. The third job in Figure 15–1 demonstrates this type of display: *grep* and *cut* have finished executing, but *anova* is still running.

jobs –l displays jobs in long format. The long format reports the process ID along with the usual information.

In *tcsh*, you can cause automatic *jobs* execution whenever you stop a job, if you set the *listjobs* shell variable in your ˜*/.cshrc* file as follows:

```
    set listjobs
```

If you would rather have *jobs –l* executed instead, set *listjobs* to *long*, as shown below:

```
    set listjobs = long
```

Finding Out When Jobs Finish

By default, when a job finishes (or otherwise changes state), the shell informs you that the job has completed only when it must print another prompt.[*] If you want

---

[*] Thus, if you start a command in the background and then just wait for the shell to tell you when the job is done, it never will. You need at least to hit RETURN every now and then to get a new prompt.

to be notified immediately, set the *notify* shell variable in your `~/.cshrc` file as shown below:

```
set notify
```

set notify provides you with quicker notification. However, if a notification message occurs in the middle of the output from another command, you might miss it in the jumble. You may not find that a problem, since you can always use *jobs* to find out if a job is still running. Try notification both ways and see which one you prefer.

The Current and Previous Jobs

jobs output indicates two special jobs: current and previous jobs. These jobs are flagged with a + and − next to the status column (see the fourth and first jobs in Figure 15−1). When a job is stopped (or put into the background, when there are no stopped jobs), it becomes the current job. Any job that was current at the time becomes the previous job. When the current job terminates, the previous job once again becomes the current job.

Changing a Job's State

A job can be moved from one state (foreground, background, or suspended) to any other state. The commands used to manipulate jobs are listed in Table 15−1; %*j* designates the job on which you wish to operate. *fg, bg, kill,* and *stop* can take multiple job specifier arguments, each of which is processed in turn. Table 15−2 shows the various forms that %*j* can take.

Table 15−1: Job Control Commands

Command	Effect of Command
CTRL-Z	Stop the foreground job
CTRL-C	Interrupt (terminate) foreground job
fg %j	Bring stopped or background job to foreground
bg %j	Move stopped job to background
kill %j	Kill (terminate) stopped or background job
stop %j	Stop background job
suspend	Suspend current shell (if non-login shell)
jobs	Display current job list

Table 15–2: Job Specifiers

Specifier	Job to Which the Specifier Refers
%	Current job (%+ and %% are synonyms for %)
%-	Previous job
%*n*	Job number *n*
%*str*	Job whose command line begins with *str*
%?*str*	Job whose command line contains *str*

You can often refer to a job more easily by name than by number, although %*str* and %?*str* are ambiguous if they match more than one job in your job list. When such a situation occurs, the shell provides warning. For example, our job list includes two jobs beginning with *vi* and two jobs containing *reference.ms*. As a result, the following commands are ambiguous:

```
% fg %vi
%vi: Ambiguous.
% fg %?ref
%?ref: Ambiguous.
```

If you use %?*str* to refer to a job and the shell responds with No match, the shell is interpreting the ? as a pattern-matching character. If that happens, try escaping the ? with a backslash, i.e., use %\?*str*. Some versions of the shell require the backslash for *fg*, *bg*, *kill*, and *stop*. Others require it only for *kill* and *stop*.

The job control commands that you use to manage jobs by moving them from one state to another are discussed in the following sections, and are summarized in Figure 15–2.

Stopping a Job

CTRL-Z stops the current foreground job. Some programs ignore CTRL-Z part of the time, e.g., *vi* cannot be stopped if you are in insert mode.

To stop a background job, use *stop*. For example, any of the following commands will stop the *grep/cut/anova* pipeline shown in Figure 15–1:

```
% stop %3
% stop %gr
% stop %?ano
```

You can also stop a background job by bringing it to the foreground (see "Resuming a Job" below), and then typing CTRL-Z.

Stopping a stopped job has no effect, as shown below:

```
% stop %1
%1: Already stopped
```

		Initial Job State		
		foreground	background	stopped
Desired Job State	foreground		`fg %j`	`fg %j`
	background	`CTRL-Z + bg %j`		`bg %j`
	stopped	`CTRL-Z`	`stop %j`	
	killed	`CTRL-C`	`kill %j`	`kill %j`

Figure 15-2: Commands that move jobs from one state to another

Beware of inadvertently starting two editing sessions on the same file. Multiple editing sessions can occur if you stop an editor and then issue a new editor command for the file, instead of resuming the editor job that you had stopped. If you switch between sessions, you can have problems because each editing job may wipe out the changes you saved in the other.

Resuming a Job

fg brings a stopped or background job to the foreground:

```
% fg %4                         Resume the second vi command
% fg %pr                        Move print job from background to foreground
```

bg restarts a stopped job in the background. If you start a command and decide that it's taking too long, you can stop it with CTRL-Z, and then use *bg* to move it to the background. At that point, you can continue working on other things.

If a background job tries to read from the terminal, it stops. Bring the job to the foreground to interact with it.

Shorthand forms of fg and bg

The *fg* and *bg* commands have some shorthand forms:

- If *fg* and *bg* are issued without a job specifier, they default to the current job.
- If you type in a job specifier by itself, the *fg* command is assumed.
- If you add a & to a specifier, *bg* is assumed instead of *fg*.

These rules are illustrated in Table 15–3.

Table 15–3: Alternate Forms of the fg and bg Commands

fg Command	Synonym(s)	bg Command	Synonym(s)
fg %	fg or %	bg %	bg or %&
fg %3	%3	bg %3	%3&
fg %pr	%pr	bg %pr	%pr&
fg %?ano	%?ano	bg %?ano	%?ano&

Killing a Job

A job can be terminated if it is stopped, or running in the foreground, or running in the background. Your interrupt character (typically CTRL–C) usually terminates the current foreground job. If a job is stopped or running in the background, use the *kill* command. For example, to kill job 5, do the following:

```
% kill %5
[5]    Terminated                   pr Results2 | lpr
```

Alternatively, bring the job to the foreground, and then type CTRL–C.

Jobs retain their assigned number. For example, if you kill job 1, jobs 2 and up are not renumbered.

Killing stubborn Jobs

Some jobs catch CTRL–C, and therefore cannot be killed by it. When this condition occurs, try stopping the job with CTRL–Z, then issue a *kill* command. Occasionally, even *kill* does not kill a job (some programs catch the signal that *kill* sends). In such cases, you can use *kill −9* to send an uncatchable signal.

Suspending a Non-Login Shell

The *suspend* job control command works only in subshells (non-login shells). It suspends the subshell and returns you to the parent shell. You can resume the subshell like any other job using *fg*.

suspend is especially useful for subshells that were started with *su*, because you need to type the password only when you start the subshell. Thereafter, you can simply move into and out of the subshell. *suspend* is even more convenient if you have one of those annoying versions of *su* that does not read the ˜/.cshrc file of the account to which you are switching. In such cases the *su* forces you to *source* it explicitly when you start the subshell. With *suspend*, you need to *source* the file only once.

To make *suspend* easier to use, put the following alias in the `~/.cshrc` of the account you're switching to:

```
alias z suspend
```

Other Applications of Job Control

This section describes other ways in which job control is useful.

Controlling Background Job Output

Putting a command in the background is handy when you want to do other things while the job is running, but the command may write output to the terminal at inconvenient times. If you are editing a file or composing a mail message, you may not want a background job to splatter output all over the screen. Or, if you have multiple background jobs, their output streams may interfere with each other. To avoid these problems, you can use the following command to force background jobs to stop when they are ready to write to the terminal:

```
% stty tostop
```

When you're ready to see the output of a background job that is stopped waiting to write, bring the job to the foreground.

To let background jobs write to the terminal at any time, use the following command:

```
% stty -tostop
```

The following command sequence illustrates the difference between *stty tostop* and *stty −tostop*:

`% stty tostop`	Turn *tostop* on
`% date &`	Run command in the background
`[1] 24980`	Shell reports the job number and the process ID
`[1] + Suspended (tty output) date`	Job stops when ready to produce output
`% fg`	Bring the job to the foreground
`date`	Shell echoes command line
`Mon Sep 12 11:59:14 CDT 1994`	Job writes output
`% stty -tostop`	Turn *tostop* off
`% date &`	Run the command in the background
`[1] 24982`	Shell prints the job number and the process ID
`Mon Sep 12 11:59:21 CDT 1994`	Job writes output without stopping
`[1]    Done       date`	Shell notifies you that the job has finished

To specify the kind of output behavior that you want for background jobs, put the appropriate *stty* command in your `~/.login` file.

Backgrounding Interactive Jobs

Interactive commands usually expect to read from and write to your terminal. Some interactive commands like *more* and *vi* are not useful in the background because they immediately try to read from the terminal and stop. But others can be put in the background during a long operation that doesn't require your attention. For example, if you are using anonymous FTP to perform a file transfer, the sequence of FTP commands might look something like the following:

```
% ftp some.machine.name
User: anonymous
Password: (type your e-mail address here)
ftp> cd pub
ftp> mode binary
ftp> get software.tar.Z
ftp> bye
```

If the get operation is slow, you may want to do other work in the meantime. Do so by running *ftp* interactively up through the get command, then stop the job and move it to the background:

```
% ftp some.machine.name
User: anonymous
Password: (type your e-mail address here)
ftp> cd pub
ftp> mode binary
ftp> get software.tar.Z
CTRL-Z
Stopped.
% bg
[1]  ftp some.machine.name &
```

Putting *ftp* in the background allows the transfer to proceed while you work on other things. After the transfer finishes, *ftp* tries to read the terminal to solicit another command from you and stops. The shell then tells you that *ftp* is waiting for you to continue typing:

```
[1]  + Stopped (tty input)  ftp some.machine.name
```

Return the job to the foreground to resume your *ftp* session:

```
% fg                            Bring ftp to the foreground
```

You should be aware of the following subtlety when you background an interactive command: the command may have already printed its next prompt by the time you resume it, and might not be smart enough to reprint the prompt again. Just go ahead and type the next input line.

Using Job Control To Improve System Response

When you have so many background jobs that the system slows down unaccept-ably, you should probably stop some of the jobs. Suppose that you start a lot of big *sort* jobs in the background:

```
% sort data1 -o data1 &
[1] 8273
% sort data2 -o data2 &
[2] 8274
    .
    .
    .
% sort data10 -o data10 &
[10] 8282
```

Shortly thereafter, your system administrator reports that everybody is complaining about how slowly the machine is running, and notes that you are the culprit. You can alleviate the situation by stopping several of the jobs:

```
% stop %2 %3 %4 %5 %6 %7 %8 %9 %10
```

After the first job finishes, start the second job running in the background again:

```
% %2 &
```

When the second job finishes, restart the third job, etc. Alternatively, you can restart the jobs in sequence, as shown below:

```
% %2 ; %3 ; %4 ; %5 ; %6 ; %7 ; %8 ; %9 ; %10
```

Job Control and Window Systems

If you are using a system that allows you to open multiple terminal windows, you can switch between windows as an alternate form of job control (e.g., if a com-mand is slow in one window, you can switch to another window). However, even if you have access to multiple windows, there are still reasons to use job control:

- Commands manipulated by job control are often related; therefore, using your history in constructing those commands can be useful. In a windowing system, the history of one window is not directly usable in another.

- Establishing new windows can be more cumbersome and slower than switch-ing between jobs in a single window.

- Starting lots of windows means that you have more of them to keep track of, move around, iconize, etc. Job control helps keep the display more manage-able by reducing clutter.

I find it more convenient to use multiple windows if I need to switch between jobs, and if each job requires a full-screen display. Otherwise, I generally find that using job control to switch between jobs in a single window is easier.

III

Appendixes

Obtaining and Installing tcsh

This appendix describes how to obtain, build, test, and install *tcsh*. As I write, *tcsh* is at version 6.06. If a more recent version has been released, simply substitute the new version number for 6.06 in the following commands in which it appears.

The first step in installing *tcsh* is determining if an up-to-date *tcsh* is already installed on your system. If so, you do not need to do anything except change your login shell to *tcsh*. (See "Selecting a Shell" in Chapter 1, *Introduction*.) Otherwise, you must obtain the current version and then install it.

Find out whether *tcsh* is installed and what its pathname is by asking your system administrator, or by running this command:

```
% which tcsh
```

If *tcsh* is present, determine its version number using the following command. Use single quotes as shown, but substitute the actual pathname if it differs from */bin/tcsh*:

```
% /bin/tcsh -c 'echo $version'
tcsh 6.00.02 (Cornell) 08/05/91 options 8b,nls,dl,al,dir
```

If the output of this command indicates that your *tcsh* is an old version (as it does in the above example), obtain the current version and install it.

Obtaining the Source Distribution

The *tcsh* source distribution is available on the Internet via anonymous FTP. Connect to *ftp.deshaw.com*, change into the */pub/tcsh* directory, and transfer the file *tcsh-6.06.tar.gz* in binary mode. After you obtain the distribution, uncompress it and extract the files:

```
% gunzip < tcsh-6.06.tar.gz | tar xf -
```

Or, on System V systems:

```
% gunzip < tcsh-6.06.tar.gz | tar xof -
```

If you don't have *gunzip*, specify the filename without the *.gz* suffix as *tcsh-6.06.tar* when you get the distribution. The FTP server will uncompress the file for you. Then run one of these commands:

```
% tar xf tcsh-6.06.tar          (For non-System V systems)
% tar xof tcsh-6.06.tar         (For System V systems)
```

The *tar* command should produce a directory *tcsh-6.06* in your current directory. Change into that directory with *cd tcsh-6.06* and you're ready to begin the build process.

If you want to use a World Wide Web browser to obtain the distribution, use the following URL:

```
ftp://ftp.deshaw.com/pub/tcsh/tcsh-6.06.tar.gz
```

Or, to obtain the uncompressed version:

```
ftp://ftp.deshaw.com/pub/tcsh/tcsh-6.06.tar
```

After you obtain the file, unpack it using the instructions above.

If you cannot reach *ftp.deshaw.com*, the distribution is also available from *ftp.gw.com* in the */pub/unix/tcsh* directory, and from *ftp.primate.wisc.edu* in the */pub/csh-tcsh-book* directory.

Build the Distribution—Quick Instructions

If you're impatient, you can try a quick build to get going sooner.

If *imake*, *xmkmf*, and the X11 configuration files are installed on your machine, you should be able to build *tcsh* like this:

```
% xmkmf                  Generate Makefile from Imakefile
% make depend            Generate dependencies (optional)
% make                   Build tcsh
```

If you're not using *imake*, create a *Makefile* from the standard template and use it to build *tcsh*:

```
% cp Makefile.std Makefile       Copy Makefile from standard template
% cp config/file config.h        Create config.h from appropriate file in config directory
% make                           Build tcsh
```

If the *make* command succeeds, you should have an executable *tcsh*, regardless of the method you use. Proceed to the section "Testing and Installing tcsh." Otherwise, use the detailed instructions in the next section to build *tcsh*.

Build the Distribution—Detailed Instructions

If the quick build doesn't work or if you want to review and perhaps modify the configuration parameters, follow the instructions given in this section. Read the entire procedure described below before you proceed.

The files that contain information about building *tcsh* are as follows:

- *README*: the general readme file
- *README.imake*: the *imake*-specific readme file
- *FAQ*: the frequently-asked-questions list
- *Ported*: the file that describes build flags for systems to which *tcsh* has been ported

I recommend that you browse through these files before proceeding.

Overview of the Build Process

Here is a summary of the steps involved in building *tcsh*:

- Decide where you want to install *tcsh*.

- Configure *Makefile*. If you are using *imake*, the *Makefile* is generated from *Imakefile* and *imake.config*; otherwise the *Makefile* is created from *Makefile.std*.

- Configure *config.h*. This file contains system-dependent configuration flags used at compile time. The file is created for you automatically if you are using *imake*; otherwise, you create *config.h* from one of the files in the *config* directory.

- Configure *config_f.h*. This file contains options that turn on or off various *tcsh* features.

- Compile *tcsh*.

As you get set up to build *tcsh*, you may need to make changes to one or more of the files mentioned above. Use the following procedure to save a copy of any file that you need to modify:

```
% cp file file.orig          Save copy of original file
% chmod 644 file             Make working copy writable so that you can modify it
```

That way, you still have the original file for reference as you modify your working copy.

Choose an Installation Directory

Before you build *tcsh*, think about where you're going to install it. The default installation directory is */usr/local/bin*, but you can override it. For example, I install *tcsh* in */bin*, so that I can use it even when the */usr* file system is unmounted.

tcsh is best installed in one of the directories in your system's standard search path, to make accessing it easy for everyone on your system. If you don't have permission to install files into any of those directories, ask your system administrator to install *tcsh* for you.

If you don't want to use the default directory, you should consider the following as you decide where to install *tcsh*:

- The build procedure compiles a pathname into the *tcsh* binary so that *tcsh* knows how to set the value of the *shell* variable properly as it starts up. You need to determine what pathname to use.

- The install commands in the *Makefile* must know where to put the *tcsh* binary; therefore, you need to tell those commands what directory to use.

In many cases, the directory used in the compiled-in pathname and for the install commands is the same. For example, you might compile a pathname of */bin/tcsh* into *tcsh* and then install the resulting binary into */bin*.

However, you might want to configure the two directories to be different. You might want the stability of being able to reference *tcsh* using a fixed name such as */bin/tcsh*, but you might also want the freedom of placing the actual binary wherever you desire, such as */usr/local/new/tcsh*. These goals can be reached by using */bin/tcsh* as the compiled-in pathname and installing *tcsh* in */usr/local/new*, and then making */bin/tcsh* a symbolic link to */usr/local/new/tcsh*. Alternatively, you might want to draw a distinction between the compiled-in pathname and the location in which *tcsh* is actually installed, if your systems run in an environment that uses NFS or AFS to share file systems over a network.

Configure the Makefile

The *Makefile* directs the build process by generating the commands needed to compile the intermediate object files and the final *tcsh* executable.

If you are using *imake*, the *Makefile* is generated from *Imakefile* and *imake.config* by running *xmkmf*. Examine *imake.config* to see if you want to make any changes. If you want to change the pathname that gets compiled into *tcsh*, define TcshPath. For example, to use */bin/tcsh*, add the following line:

```
#define TcshPath /bin/tcsh
```

To change the directory used by the installation commands, define `DestBin` as follows:

```
#define DestBin /bin
```

The manual page is installed by default as */usr/local/man/man1/tcsh.1*. If you want to change this location, define `DestMan` as the installation directory and `Man-Suffix` as the extension used for the file in that directory. For example, to install *tcsh.man* as */usr/man/mann/tcsh.n*, add the following lines to *imake.config*:

```
#define DestMan /usr/man/mann
#define ManSuffix n
```

After you've looked through *imake.config* and made the appropriate changes, create the *Makefile* and generate the source file dependencies as shown below:[*]

```
% xmkmf                 Generate Makefile
% make depend           Generate dependencies (optional)
```

If you are not using *imake*, the configuration process is different. First, create a *Makefile* with which to work by copying the template *Makefile.std*:

```
% cp Makefile.std Makefile    Copy working Makefile from Makefile.std
% chmod 644 Makefile          Make it writable
```

Then, edit *Makefile* to choose the appropriate configuration parameters for your system. The *Makefile* has a lot of information about the settings for different systems, and you can also read *Ported* to see what special flags might be necessary for your machine. (The systems for a given vendor do not necessarily appear together in *Ported*; be sure to look completely through it to find the best match for your system.)

The most important configuration parameters are listed below. Make sure you look at the possible settings in the *Makefile* and select those which are most appropriate for your system:

CC   The C compiler

DFLAGS   –D's and –U's to pass to the C compiler

LDFLAGS   Loader (linker) flags

LIBES   Link libraries

CFLAGS   Special flags to pass to the C compiler

For each parameter, there may be several possible settings described in the *Make-file*. A leading # character is used to make every setting a comment except one, which is the default setting. To select a different setting, put a # in front of the default and remove the leading # from the setting you want to use.

---

[*] If you modify either *Imakefile* or *imake.config* later, you'll need to rerun *xmkmf* and *make depend* to bring the *Makefile* and the dependencies up to date again.

If you are going to install *tcsh* in a location other than the default location, you need to make two changes to the *Makefile*. Suppose you want to install *tcsh* as */bin/tcsh*. First, set the pathname that gets compiled into the *tcsh* binary. Find the DFLAGS line that you are using and add to it a definition for the _PATH_TCSHELL macro. If the DFLAGS line looks like this:

```
DFLAGS=
```

then change it to appear as shown below (be sure to type the quotes exactly as shown):

```
DFLAGS= -D_PATH_TCSHELL='"/bin/tcsh"'
```

(If DFLAGS has a non-empty value, simply add -D_PATH_TCSHELL='"/bin/tcsh"' to the end of the existing value.)

Second, set the directory to be used by the installation commands when you install *tcsh*. Look for the line that sets the DESTBIN variable:

```
DESTBIN = $(TCSHTOP)/bin
```

Change that line to this:

```
DESTBIN = /bin
```

To change the point at which the manual page is installed, set DESTMAN to the installation directory and MANSECT to the file extension in that directory. To install *tcsh.man* as */usr/man/mann/tcsh.n*, the settings should look like these:

```
DESTMAN = /usr/man/mann
MANSECT = n
```

Configure config.h

config.h contains some general system-dependent configuration flags used at compile time. *config.h* is from one of the files in the *config* directory.

If you use *imake*, you don't need to create *config.h*. The *Makefile* generated from the *Imakefile* includes a command that creates *config.h* by selecting the proper file from the *config* directory.

If you're not using *imake*, examine the *config* directory and determine which one of the files is most appropriate for your system. Then, copy the file into the main *tcsh* distribution directory as *config.h*. For example, the *hpux8* file works for both HP-UX 8.xx and 9.xx. On my HP 715 running HP-UX 9.05, I do the following:

```
% cp config/hpux8 config.h        Create config.h from vendor file
% chmod 644 config.h              Make config.h writable
```

Normally, you won't need to modify *config.h*, but you should examine it in case there are minor tweaks that would be helpful. (If you do modify *config.h* first, make a copy of it for reference, because the original will be removed if you run *make clean* later.)

Configure config_f.h

config_f.h contains several compilation flags that turn on or off various *tcsh* capabilities. Examine it to see if you want to change any of the flags. For example, if you do not have *locale.h* on your system and cannot compile in Native Language System (NLS) support, turn on that feature by changing the following line:

    #define NLS

to this:

    #undef NLS

If you want the *tcsh* command editor to default to the *vi* key bindings instead of the *emacs* bindings, change the following line:

    #undef VIDEFAULT

to this:

    #define VIDEFAULT

Compile tcsh

After you've edited the build files so that they have the correct configuration parameters, generate *tcsh* as shown below:

    % make

If the *make* command does not generate an executable *tcsh*, take a look at the last half of the *README* file to see if there are known workarounds for the problems that occur. Also, read the *FAQ* file and examine *Ported* to see if you overlooked any flags that are needed for building *tcsh* on your system.

If you're having *imake* problems, contact me at *dubois@primate.wisc.edu*.

Porting tcsh to a New System

If *tcsh* has not been compiled on the kind of system that you have, you may not be able to find the appropriate configuration information for your machine. In that case, try to make educated guesses based on the parameter values from systems that are closest to yours. You may also want to add a new entry to *host.defs*, which describes how to set some system-related environment variables.

After you're done, please send your changes to *tcsh@mx.gw.com* so that they can be incorporated into future releases.

Testing and Installing tcsh

After building *tcsh*, you should test it as shown below:

```
% ./tcsh              Start the tcsh you just built
% ...run some commands...   See how it works
% exit                Terminate it
```

Point eight of the *README* file suggests some special commands that you can use to exercise *tcsh*. You should try doing some everyday work with the newly built shell, to see how it performs under ordinary circumstances.

When you're satisfied that *tcsh* is stable, install the binary and the manual page using the following commands:

```
% make install        Install the tcsh binary
% make install.man    Install the manual page
```

If you encounter problems, try to determine the circumstances under which they occur. Consult the *README* and *FAQ* files, and verify by looking in *Ported* that you compiled *tcsh* with all special flags needed on your system.

Allowing tcsh To Be a Login Shell

After you have installed *tcsh*, you're almost finished. The final step is to make sure that *tcsh* can be used as a login shell. Typically, you select a login shell using a command like *chsh* or *passwd −s*. These commands will likely require that *tcsh* be registered with the system as a trusted shell. Also, your FTP server may reject connections to accounts that have *tcsh* as the login shell unless *tcsh* is registered as a trusted shell.

The most common method of informing the system of which shells are trusted is the */etc/shells* file. Determine if a *getusershell*(3) manual page exists to find out if this is true for you. Typically, the trusted shell list is determined as follows:

- If */etc/shells* exists, the shells listed in it are considered trusted login shells. If */etc/shells* is already present on your system, you only need to add the *tcsh* pathname to it.

- If */etc/shells* does not exist, there is a set of shells that the system considers to be trusted login shells by default. (The *getusershell*(3) manual page should indicate which shells are in this set.) In order to register *tcsh*, you must create */etc/shells* and then add the pathname for *tcsh* as well as the paths of all the default shells. If you put only *tcsh* in the file, then the default shells will no longer be considered trusted!

Entries in */etc/shells* must be full pathnames. The following is an example from one of my systems:

```
/bin/sh
/bin/csh
/bin/ksh
/bin/tcsh
```

After modifying */etc/shells*, try changing your login shell to *tcsh* to verify that the system accepts it. You should also be able to use *ftp* to connect to your machine with your regular login name and password, as shown:

```
% ftp yourhost
Name: yourname
Password: yourpassword
```

If Your System Does Not Use /etc/shells

Some systems use a file other than */etc/shells* to identify which shells are considered legal, and the file may have a different format. For example, */etc/shells* is replaced under AIX by the `shell =` line in */etc/security/login.cfg*. Consult your local documentation for more specific information.

B

csh and tcsh
Quick Reference

This appendix briefly summarizes shell features and characteristics. Examples and additional commentary may be found elsewhere in this handbook. See also the *csh* and *tcsh* manual pages.

Command Structure

A simple command (designated *cmd* below) consists of a command name, possibly followed by one or more arguments. This basic form may be modified or combined with other commands to form more complex command sequences:

`cmd`	Run *cmd*
`cmd &`	Run *cmd* in the background
`cmd > file`	Write *cmd* output to *file* (overwrites *file*)
`cmd >> file`	Write *cmd* output to *file* (appends to *file*)
`cmd < file`	Take *cmd* input from *file*
`cmd1 ; cmd2`	Run *cmd1*, then *cmd2*
`cmd1	cmd2`	Write *cmd1* output to input of *cmd2*
`(cmd1 ; cmd2)`	Run *cmd1* and *cmd2* in subshell
`cmd1 ` `cmd2` `	Use *cmd2* to produce arguments for *cmd1*

Startup and Shutdown Files

The shell reads one or more files from your home directory when it starts up, and possibly one file when it terminates. The files are described in the following table. No error occurs if any given file does not exist.

File	Description
˜/.cshrc	Read at startup
˜/.tcshrc	Read instead of ˜/.cshrc if it exists (*tcsh* only—if you're using *tcsh*, read references to ˜/.cshrc as "˜/.tcshrc if it exists, ˜/.cshrc otherwise.")
˜/.login	Read by login shells at startup
˜/.history	Read by login shells at startup to initialize the history list
˜/.cshdirs	Read by login shells at startup to initialize the directory stack (*tcsh* only)
˜/.logout	Read by login shells at termination

At startup, a login shell reads, in order, ˜/.cshrc, ˜/.history, ˜/.login, and (for *tcsh* only) ˜/.cshdirs. A non-login shell reads only ˜/.cshrc at startup.

At termination, a login shell reads ˜/.logout and writes ˜/.history and (for *tcsh* only) ˜/.cshdirs if the appropriate variables are set. (˜/.history is saved if *savehist* is set. In *tcsh*, ˜/.cshdirs is saved if *savedirs* is set.) A non-login shell simply exits.

To execute commands in ˜/.cshrc that will only apply to interactive shells, place them inside the following construct:

```
if ($?prompt) then
    commands
endif
```

To execute commands only for *tcsh*, place them inside this construct:

```
if ($?tcsh) then
    commands
endif
```

Variables

There are two types of variables: shell variables and environment variables. Shell variables are available only to the shell in which they are defined. Environment variables are available to the current shell and also to other processes (including subshells) that are started from the shell. By convention, shell variables are lowercase and environment variables are uppercase.

Some useful shell variables are listed in the table below.

Variable	Description
autologout	If set, automatic logout occurs after you have been inactive for an hour. If set to a number, logout occurs after that many minutes of inactivity. Some shells set *autologout* by default at login time. To disable, unset *autologout* in ˜/.cshrc.

Variable	Description
cdpath	A list of directories in which the shell looks for directories specified as arguments to *cd* or *pushd*.
correct	If set to cmd, turns on spelling correction for command names. If set to all, turns on spelling correction for the entire command line (*tcsh* only).
cwd	Set by the shell to your current working directory when your directory changes.
fignore	A list of filename suffixes. Filenames ending with any of the suffixes are ignored for filename completion.
filec	In *csh*, turns on filename completion. (Unnecessary for *tcsh*.)
history	If set, specifies the number of commands to save in the history list.
home	The pathname to your home directory.
ignoreeof	If set, CTRL-D does not terminate the shell. You need to explicitly type *exit* or *logout*.
mail	Pathname of file to check periodically to see if new mail has arrived.
notify	If set, the shell notifies you immediately when background jobs finish. Otherwise it waits until just before the next prompt.
path	A list of directories in which the shell looks for commands.
prompt	Your prompt string. Set only by interactive shells. Can be tested to distinguish interactive from non-interactive shells.
rmstar	If set, *tcsh* asks "if you really mean it" when it sees * given as an argument to the *rm* command (*tcsh* only).
savedirs	If set, login shells save the directory stack in ˜/.*cshdirs* when you log out. The stack is read back in when you log in again (*tcsh* only).
savehist	If set, login shells save the history list in ˜/.*history* when you log out. The history list is read back in when you log in again.
shell	The pathname of your login shell.
tcsh	Set to *tcsh* version number (*tcsh* only; can be tested to distinguish *tcsh* from *csh*).
term	Your terminal type.
user	Your user (login) name.
version	Shell version and configuration information (*tcsh* only).

Many environment variables (such as *HOME, PATH, SHELL, TERM,* and *USER*) are used like the corresponding shell variables with lowercase names. Other useful environment variables are listed in the table below.

Variable	Description
DISPLAY	Display specification used by X Window System.
EDITOR	Pathname of your preferred editor.
HOST	The current machine name (*tcsh* only).
LOGNAME	Like *USER*.

Variable	Description
PWD	Like *cwd*.
VISUAL	Pathname of your preferred full-screen editor.

Defining, Removing, and Examining Variables

You can define shell and environment variables, examine their values, or remove them as indicated below.

Command	Description
set *var*	Define shell variable, no value (just turn it on)
set *var* = *value*	Define shell variable with explicit value
set *var* = (*str1 str2 str3*)	Define shell variable with value consisting of multiple strings
setenv *VAR value*	Define environment variable
set	Display all shell variable values
setenv	Display all environment variable values
unset *var*	Remove shell variable
unsetenv *VAR*	Remove environment variable

A read-only shell variable can be defined using *set −r* instead of *set*. Read-only variables cannot be modified or removed.

Shell variables are usually set in ˜/.cshrc. Environment variables are usually set in ˜/.login.

Using Variables

To use a variable, refer to it as $*name* or ${*name*}. Modifiers can be applied to a variable reference (as $*name:m* or ${*name:m*}) to extract part of the variable's value.

Modifier	Description
r	Root of value (everything but extension following dot)
e	Extension of value (suffix following dot)
h	Head of value (all but last pathname component)
t	Tail of value (last pathname component)

Special Characters

Several characters have special meaning to the shell.

Character(s)	Description
* ? [ ] ^ { } ~	Filename pattern matching and expansion
$	Variable reference
|	Pipe
< >	Input and output redirection
! ^	History reference and quick substitution
&	Background execution
;	Command separator
SPACE	Argument separator
TAB	Filename completion (*tcsh*)
ESC	Filename completion (*csh*)
(...)	Subshell execution
`...`	Command substitution
\ ' "	Quote characters

Special Characters in Filenames

Filename arguments can contain the following special characters in order to do pattern matching or home-directory substitution.

Character(s)	Description
*	Match an arbitrary length sequence of characters
?	Match a single character
[...]	Match any character named between brackets
[^...]	Match any character not named between brackets (*tcsh* only)
^*pattern*	Match filenames not matching *pattern* (*tcsh* only)
{...}	String expansion operator
~	Expands to pathname of your home directory
~*name*	Expands to pathname of home directory for user *name*

Quote Characters

Quote characters turn off any special meaning a character has, allowing it be used as an ordinary character.

Character(s)	Description
\	Quote the following character.
'...'	Quote the characters between single quotes. !*event* is still evaluated as a history substitution.

Character(s)	Description
`"..."`	Quote the characters between double quotes. `!event`, `$var`, and `` `cmd` `` are still evaluated as history, variable, and command substitutions.

Command History

The shell's history mechanism allows you to recall previous events (commands) and then repeat them. To enable command history, set the *history* shell variable in `~/.cshrc` to the number of events that you want the shell to remember. To preserve your history across logins, set the *savehist* shell variable.

The *history* command displays your current history:

`history`	Display entire history list
`history n`	Display last *n* events from history list

History Event Specifiers

History references begin with a `!` character. When the shell sees such a reference, it replaces it in the command line, echoes the resulting command, and executes it.

The event specifiers listed below select commands from the history list:

Specifier	Description
`!!`	Repeat previous command
`!n`	Repeat command *n*
`!-n`	Repeat *n*-th-to-last command
`!str`	Repeat last command beginning with `str`
`!?str?`	Repeat last command containing `str`
`!#`	Repeat the current command line typed so far

Word Designators

The word designators listed below extract particular words from an event:

Designator	Description
`0`	Word 0 (the command name)
`n`	Word *n* (argument *n*)
`^`	Word 1
`$`	Last word
`m-n`	Words *m* through *n*
`-n`	Words 0 through *n*
`m-`	Words *m* through (but not including) last word

Designator	Description
–	Words 0 through (but not including) last word
m*	Words *m* through last word
*	Words 1 through last word, or empty if there are no arguments
%	Following a !?*str*? event specifier, the word matched by *str*

Word designators are usually separated from the preceding event specifier by a colon. However, some shortcuts may be used: if a designator begins with *, ^, $, or %, you can omit the colon; if you apply a designator to the previous command (!!), you can shorten !! to !; and you can designate all arguments, the first argument, or the last argument of the previous command using !*, !^, or !$.

History Modifiers

To fix or change a word from the previous command, use ^*old*^*new*:

```
% mroe file1 file2 file3
mroe: Command not found.
% ^ro^or
more file1 file2 file3
```

Other modifiers are listed below. They are appended to history references that begin with !, and are separated from the reference by a colon.

Modifier	Description
r	Root of filename (everything but extension following dot)
e	Extension of filename (suffix following dot)
h	Head of pathname (all but last component)
t	Tail of pathname (last component)
s/*old*/*new*/	Perform substitution, replacing *old* with *new*
&	Repeat previous s substitution
g	Apply modifier following g globally to each word
p	Print resulting command without executing it
q	Quote words (prevents filename pattern expansion)
x	Like q but break into words at whitespace
u	Make first lowercase letter uppercase (*tcsh* only)
l	Make first uppercase letter lowercase (*tcsh* only)
a	Apply modifier(s) following a as many times as possible to a word. If used with g, a is applied to all words. (*tcsh* only)

Moving Around the File System

To move around the file system, you specify a directory name as the argument to a directory-changing command. The directories shown below have special names.

Name	Description
.	Current directory
..	Parent of current directory
~	Your home directory
~name	Home directory for user *name*

The *cd* command changes to a given directory, which becomes your current directory:

cd	Move to your home directory
cd dir1	Move down one level to *dir1*
cd dir1/dir2	Move down two levels, through *dir1* to *dir2*
cd ..	Move up one level to parent directory
cd ../..	Move up two levels to parent of parent
cd ../dir3	Move up a level, then back down to *dir3*
cd /	Move to root directory (top of file system)
cd ~dubois	Move to home directory of *dubois* account
cd -	Move to last location (*tcsh* only)

The shell maintains a directory stack. Stack entries are numbered, starting from 0. *pushd* and *popd* change directory (like *cd*), but they also add and remove entries from the stack as shown below:

pushd *dir*	Add *dir* to stack and change to it
pushd	Exchange top two stack entries
pushd +*n*	Rotate stack so entry *n* is on top
popd	Drop top entry and return to previous entry
popd +*n*	Drop entry *n* entry from stack (*tcsh*, some versions of *csh*)

The *dirs* command displays or clears the directory stack:

dirs	Display stack
dirs -l	Display stack using long names (no ~*name* abbreviations)
dirs -n	Display stack, wrapping output (*tcsh* only)
dirs -v	Display stack, including entry numbers, one line per entry (*tcsh* only)
dirs -c	Clear stack (*tcsh* only)

In *tcsh*, the −*l*, −*n*, and −*v* flags can also be used with *cd*, *pushd*, and *popd*, and have the same meaning as for *dirs*.

In *tcsh*, typing =*n* at the beginning of a command argument is equivalent to typing the value of stack entry *n*. =− refers to the final entry. Filename completion may be used with arguments that begin with =*n*/ or =−/.

Aliases

Aliases allow short names to be given to commands or command sequences. Invoking the alias name is equivalent to invoking the corresponding commands. To create or display alias definitions, or to remove aliases, use the following commands:

alias *name definition*	Define alias *name*
alias *name*	Display definition for alias *name*
alias	Display all alias definitions
unalias *name*	Remove alias *name*
unalias *	Remove all aliases

If a definition contains special characters, it should be quoted.

When you invoke an alias, any arguments are added to the end of the command to which the alias expands. To place arguments at a specific location within the command, use one of the following sequences in the alias definition.

Sequence	Description
\!*	All arguments
\!^	First argument
\!$	Last argument
\!:*n*	Argument *n*

Filename Completion

To use filename completion, type a prefix of a filename and hit the completion key. If the prefix is unique, the shell types the rest of the filename for you. Otherwise, it types as much as is common to all matches, and then beeps. In *tcsh*, the completion key is TAB and filename completion is always active. In *csh*, the completion key is ESC; in addition, you must set the *filec* variable in ˜/.cshrc to turn on filename completion.

To list completion matches for a prefix (e.g., when the prefix is ambiguous), type CTRL–D.

Words beginning with ˜ are completed as home directory references. In *tcsh*, words beginning with $ are completed as variable names and words beginning with =*n* are completed as though they began with the directory named by directory stack *n*.

Setting the *fignore* shell variable to a list of filename suffixes causes names ending in those suffixes to be ignored for completion.

Programmed Completion

tcsh allows programmed completions to be specified using the *complete* command, as shown below:

```
complete command word/pattern/list/suffix
```

command is the command to which the completion applies. The argument following the command is a completion rule that specifies how to complete a word or words from the command. Although the delimiter between parts of a completion rule is often a dash, it can be any character.

There may be more than one completion rule. Each rule has the parts listed below.

Part	Description
word	Specifies how to select words from the command. It must be p, c, n, C, or N (described below).
pattern	Determines to which words the rule applies.
list	The word list from which to choose completions. The available lists are described below.
suffix	An optional suffix to be added to completed words. If missing, a slash is added to completed directory names and a space otherwise. If present, should be a single character. If the character is the same as the delimiter between parts of the completion rule, no suffix is added to completed words.

The *word* specifier determines how *pattern* is interpreted. If *word* is p, *pattern* indicates the word position or positions to which the rule applies. Otherwise, *pattern* is a filename pattern and the rule applies to any word whose leftmost part is matched by the pattern.

word	Description
p	Position-based completion. *pattern* is a number or range of numbers specifying to which words the rule applies:
	n Word *n*
	m-n Words *m* through *n*
	m* Words *m* through last word
	* All words
c	Complete the current word (the word matched by *pattern*). The part matched by the pattern is not considered part of the prefix to be completed.
n	Complete the next word after the word matched by *pattern*.
C	Complete the current word. Unlike c, the entire word is used as the prefix to be completed.

word	Description
N	Complete the word occurring two words after the word matched by *pattern*.

The word lists from which completions can be chosen are listed below.

List	Description
a	Alias names
b	Key binding names (command-line editor commands)
c	Command names
d	Directory names
e	Environment variable names
f	Filenames (any type, including directory names)
g	Group names
j	Jobs names
l	Resource limit names
n	Null list (suppresses completion)
s	Shell variable names
S	Signal names
t	Plain text filenames (actually, any non-directory)
v	Variable names (any type)
u	User names
X	Command names for which completions have been defined
x	Explain; like n, but print a message when you type CTRL-D
C, D, F, T	Like c, d, f, t, but select completion from a given directory
(*list*)	Select completion from words in the given list
$*variable*	Select completion from words in the value of the variable
`` `command` ``	Select completion from words in the output of the command

Job Control

Job control allows you to suspend or terminate jobs, or move jobs between the foreground and background. Job control commands are shown below. When used, %*j* indicates the job of interest.

Command	Description
CTRL-Z	Stop the foreground job
CTRL-C	Interrupt (terminate) foreground job
fg %*j*	Bring stopped or background job to foreground
bg %*j*	Move stopped job to background
kill %*j*	Kill (terminate) stopped or background job
stop %*j*	Stop background job
suspend	Suspend current shell (if non-login shell)
jobs	Display current job list

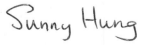

The job specifier `%j` has the following forms.

Specifier	Description
`%`	Current job (`%+` and `%%` are synonyms for `%`)
`%-`	Previous job
`%n`	Job number `n`
`%str`	Job whose command line begins with `str`
`%?str`	Job whose command line contains `str` (if shell says `No match`, use `%\?str`)

The *fg* and *bg* commands have the shorthand forms listed below.

Specifier	Description
`%j`	Equivalent to `fg %j`
`fg` or `%`	Equivalent to `fg %`
`%j&`	Equivalent to `bg %j`
`bg` or `%&`	Equivalent to `bg %`

If the *notify* shell variable is set, the shell notifies you immediately when background jobs finish. Otherwise, notification occurs when the next prompt is printed.

Use *stty* to specify whether or not background jobs can write to your terminal, as shown below:

`stty tostop`	Force background jobs to stop when ready to write to terminal
`stty -tostop`	Allow background jobs to write to terminal

Command Editing in tcsh

tcsh lets you interactively browse up and down through your history list, selecting and editing commands before executing them.

Use CTRL-P and CTRL-N (or up arrow and down arrow) to move up and down through your history list. Each recalled command is displayed on the current command line. To execute the command, hit RETURN. To cancel it, hit CTRL-C.

To edit commands, *tcsh* provides a command line editor that uses *emacs*-like or *vi*-like key bindings. Select the appropriate set using *bindkey -e* or *bindkey -v*. Some of the most useful editing commands are shown in the rest of this section. (Use *bindkey* with no arguments to see all your key bindings.)

emacs Mode Editing Commands

In *emacs* mode, characters are inserted into the command line unless they are editing commands. You can move the cursor or delete characters using the commands shown below.

Cursor motion commands

Command	Description
CTRL-B	Move cursor back (left) one character
CTRL-F	Move cursor forward (right) one character
ESC b	Move cursor back one word
ESC f	Move cursor forward one word
CTRL-A	Move cursor to beginning of line
CTRL-E	Move cursor to end of line

Text deletion commands

Command	Description
DEL or CTRL-H	Delete character to left of cursor
CTRL-D	Delete character under cursor
ESC d	Delete word
ESC DEL or ESC CTRL-H	Delete word backward
CTRL-K	Delete from cursor to end of line
CTRL-U	Delete entire line

Preceding a command with ESC n repeats the command n times.

To search up through your history list for a command containing a string, type the string and then ESC p. The matching command is pulled into the edit buffer. To search down, type a string and ESC n. The string can contain filename pattern characters. To repeat the search, simply type ESC p or ESC n.

vi Mode Editing Commands

There are two editing modes with the *vi* bindings. In insert mode, all characters (with a few exceptions, listed below) are inserted into the command line. In command mode, characters are interpreted as editing commands.

Hit ESC in insert mode to enter command mode. In command mode, several commands enter insert mode until you type ESC. If you don't know which mode you are in, hit ESC until *tcsh* beeps, and then you will be in command mode.

Some common commands for both modes are shown below.

Cursor motion commands (insert mode)

Command	Description
CTRL-B	Move cursor back (left) one character
CTRL-F	Move cursor forward (right) one character
CTRL-A	Move cursor to beginning of line

Command	Description
CTRL-E	Move cursor to end of line

Text deletion commands (insert mode)

Command	Description
DEL or CTRL-H	Delete character to left of cursor
CTRL-W	Delete word backward
CTRL-U	Delete from beginning of line to cursor
CTRL-K	Delete from cursor to end of line

Cursor motion commands (command mode)

Command	Description
w	Move cursor right one word
b	Move cursor left one word
e	Move cursor to next word ending
W, B, E	Like w, b, and e, but different word definition
^ or CTRL-A	Move cursor to beginning of line (first non-whitespace character)
0	Move cursor to beginning of line
$ or CTRL-E	Move cursor to end of line

w, b, and e stop at whitespace or punctuation. W, B, and E stop at whitespace only.

Character-seeking motion commands (command mode)

Command	Description
fc	Move cursor to next instance of c in line
Fc	Move cursor to previous instance of c in line
tc	Move cursor up to next instance of c in line
Tc	Move cursor back to previous instance of c in line
;	Repeat previous f or F command
,	Repeat previous f or F command in opposite direction

Text insertion commands (command mode)

Command	Description
a	Append new text after cursor until ESC
i	Insert new text before cursor until ESC
A	Append new text after end of line until ESC
I	Insert new text before beginning of line until ESC

Text deletion commands (command mode)

Command	Description
x	Delete character under cursor
X or DEL	Delete character to left of cursor
d*m*	Delete from cursor to end of motion command *m*
D	Synonym for d$
CTRL-W	Delete word backward
CTRL-U	Delete from beginning of line to cursor
CTRL-K	Delete from cursor to end of line

Text replacement commands (command mode)

Command	Description
c*m*	Change characters from cursor to end of motion command *m* until ESC
C	Synonym for c$
r*c*	Replace character under cursor with character *c*
R	Replace multiple characters until ESC
s	Substitute character under cursor with characters typed until ESC

In *vi* command mode, you can repeat most commands. Simply type the repeat count before the command, e.g., 3dw to delete three words.

To search up through your history list in *vi* command mode, type ? followed by a string, then RETURN. To search down, use /. The command containing the string is retrieved into the edit buffer. The string can contain filename pattern characters. To repeat a search in the same or opposite direction, use n or N.

The bindkey Command

bindkey is used to select, examine, and define key bindings. It has several forms:

bindkey -e	Select *emacs* bindings
bindkey -v	Select *vi* bindings
bindkey -d	Restore default bindings
bindkey -u	Display *bindkey* usage message
bindkey -l	List editing commands and their meanings
bindkey	List all key bindings
bindkey *key*	List binding for *key*
bindkey *key cmd*	Bind *key* to editing command *cmd*
bindkey -c *key cmd*	Bind *key* to UNIX command *cmd*
bindkey -s *key str*	Bind *key* to string *str*
bindkey -r *key*	Remove binding for *key*

bindkey –l displays a full list of editing command names along with short descriptions of each. Appendix C, *Other Sources of Information*, references a document that describes the command meanings in more detail.

The flags listed below modify the interpretation of the *key* argument. *−k* and *−b* cannot both be used in the same command.

Flag	Description
-a	Key binding applies to alternate key map (*vi* command mode key map)
-k	Allows *key* to be up, down, left, or right to indicate an arrow key
-b	Allows *key* to be C-*X* or M-*X* to indicate CTRL-*X* or META-*X*
--	If *key* begins with -, a preceding -- flag tells *bindkey* not to process *key* as a flag

Characters in the *key* argument may be ordinary characters, or one of the sequences listed below to specify special characters.

Sequence	Character Represented by Sequence
^*X*	CTRL-*X*
^[	ESC
^?	DEL
\\^	^
\\a	CTRL-G (bell)
\\b	CTRL-H
\\e	ESC
\\f	FORMFEED
\\n	NEWLINE
\\r	RETURN
\\t	TAB
\\v	CTRL-K (vertical tab)
nnn	ASCII character with octal code *nnn*

The caret sequences have their special meaning whether quoted or unquoted. The backslash in backslash sequences must be doubled if the sequence is unquoted.

c for *c* not shown above produces a literal *c*. CTRL-V CTRL-*X* produces a literal CTRL-*X*.

The same sequences may be used for the *cmd* and *str* arguments of *bindkey −c* and *bindkey −s*, except that sequences beginning with a caret are interpreted literally inside quotes.

Other Sources of Information

This appendix provides references to other sources of information about *csh* and *tcsh*.

Documents

The documents listed below are available from various places around the Internet. For your convenience, I've gathered the documents into a single location, to which I'll refer as "the archive." You can access the archive with a World Wide Web browser using the following URL:

```
http://www.primate.wisc.edu/software/csh-tcsh-book/index.html
```

Via anonymous FTP, connect to *ftp.primate.wisc.edu* and find the */pub/csh-tcsh-book* directory. Gopher clients can connect to *gopher.primate.wisc.edu*, select the "Primate Center Software Archives" item, and then select "Using csh & tcsh".

The archive contains the following documents:

* *Using csh & tcsh—Errata.* The errata sheet for this handbook.

* *tcsh*(1). The *tcsh* manual page, from the *tcsh* source distribution. Based on the 4.4BSD *csh* manual page, but revised extensively for *tcsh*. There is also a *perl* script that converts the manual page to HTML form so that you can read it using a World Wide Web browser. This form allows you to skip around by topic.

* *csh*(1). The *csh* manual page. You may already have an online version available via the *man csh* command. The version in the archive is taken from the 4.4BSD distribution.

* *An introduction to the C shell.* A general introduction written by the C shell's author. Often included in the "UNIX papers" section of UNIX system documentation. The version in the archive is taken from the 4.4BSD distribution.

- *complete.tcsh*. A file from the *tcsh* source distribution containing many examples of programmed completions.

- *tcsh Command Editor Commands*. A supplement to Chapter 7, *The tcsh Command-Line Editor*. Describes the *tcsh* command line editor command names. Similar to *bindkey −l* output, but less terse.

- *Csh programming considered harmful*. This document explains why *csh* and *tcsh* are not suitable for script writing. Note that much of this document is devoted to enumerating bugs in *csh*, most of which are fixed in *tcsh*.

- *Csh Startup Summary*. Discusses strategies that you can use to set up your ˜/.cshrc and ˜/.login startup files.

- *Xterm Control Sequences*. Describes the control sequences that you can send to *xterm*. You may already have this document in one of the following files if you have the X11 source distribution:

mit/clients/xterm/ctlseqs.ms	Location in X11R5 distribution
xc/doc/specs/xterm/ctlseqs.ms	Location in X11R6 distribution

The archive also contains command fragments and short programs for such things as setting window titles. Chapter 14, *Keeping Track of Where You Are*, describes how these are used.

Newsgroups

The Usenet newsgroup *comp.unix.shell* serves as a clearinghouse for all sorts of shell questions. If you have a problem with the shell that you suspect is peculiar to a particular vendor's implementation, one of the other *comp.unix*.* groups or one of the *comp.sys*.* groups may also be useful.

Mailing Lists

There are three mailing lists for *tcsh*.

To report bugs, send a message to *tcsh-bugs@mx.gw.com*. You need not be a member of *tcsh-bugs* to send such mail, but please be sure that what you are reporting is a bug and not simply something that you do not understand. *tcsh-bugs* is not for general *tcsh* consulting. Therefore, don't send "how do I . . . ?" or "how does . . . work?" questions; such questions will go unanswered. The *comp.unix.shell* newsgroup is a better forum for general consulting questions.

The *tcsh* and *tcsh-diffs* mailing lists are for developers who want to help maintain *tcsh* (discuss and implement new features and fix bugs). The two lists are related. *tcsh-diffs* subscribers get all the *tcsh* list traffic, but also receive patches for each development release.

To subscribe to any of these lists, send a message to *listserv@mx.gw.com*. The body of the message (not the subject line), should contain one of the following lines:

```
subscribe tcsh-bugs Your Name
subscribe tcsh Your Name
subscribe tcsh-diffs Your Name
```

Substitute your real name for *Your Name*.

Index

\ (backslash)
    as command-line continuation character,
        8, 119
    as escape for special characters, 128
    as quote character, 89, 195
^^ history operator, 25

:a history modifier, 71
adding text in vi mode, 83
addresses, UUCP (see UUCP addresses)
addsuffix shell variable, 112
alias command, 95-101, 199
"Alias loop" error, 96
aliases, 26-27, 95-101, 199
    navigating filesystem with, 155
    referring to history in, 97
    removing, 96
    and variables, 156
    and xargs command, 145
"Already stopped" error, 173
"Ambiguous" error, 173
ampersand (&), 13
    :& history modifier, 71
angle brackets < > (see less than; greater
    than), 8
apostrophe (see quotation mark)
appending output to files, 9
arguments, command, 8
arrow keys, 23, 25
    and command editor, 76, 80, 86
asterisk (*) as pattern-matching operator, 10,
    104
at sign (@), 54
autolist shell variable, 114
autologout shell variable, 192

background, 170, 172, 178
    controlling job output, 176
    interactive jobs in, 177
    running commands in, 13, 33
    stopping jobs in, 34
backquote (`) and command substitution,
    27, 138
backslash (\)
    as command-line continuation character,
        8, 119
    as escape for special characters, 128
    as quote character, 89, 195
BACKSPACE character, 8

(see also CTRL-H character)
"Bad ! arg selector" error, 97
bang (!), 59
    in filenames, 132
    in history reference, 23
    in prompt, 30, 60
bg command, 33, 172, 201
    alternate forms for, 174
bindings, 86-93, 205-206
    between key and itself, 91
    changing, 91
    for commands, 76-77
    conflicts with, 93
    displaying all, 88
    selecting, 87
        emacs, 77
        vi, 80
    specifying key argument, 89-90
bindkey command, 49, 86-93, 205-206
    -- option, 87
    -a option, 86, 89, 91
    -b option, 86, 90
    -c option, 92
    -d option, 87
    default bindings, 76
    -e option, 76, 87
    -k option, 86, 90
    -l option, 77, 87
    -r option, 92
    -s option, 92
    -v option, 76, 87
brackets < > (see less than; greater than)
brackets [ ] as pattern-matching operator,
    10, 105
brackets { }
    generating arguments with, 19
    as pattern-matching operator, 108-109

canceling commands, 76
caret (^) as pattern-matching operator, 106
case sensitivity, 10
cd command, 11, 147-148, 198
    - option, 28, 148
    idioms for, 12
cdpath shell variable, 30, 153-155, 192
changing directories, 147-157
characters
    control, in filenames, 132
    erasing, 8, 52

About the Author

Paul DuBois is a programmer at the Wisconsin Regional Primate Research Center at the University of Wisconsin-Madison. He leads a quiet life with few interests outside of family, church, and programming.

Colophon

Our look is the result of reader comments, our own experimentation, and feedback from distribution channels.

Distinctive covers complement our distinctive approach to technical topics, breathing personality and life into potentially dry subjects. UNIX and its attendant programs can be unruly beasts. Nutshell Handbooks help you tame them.

The animal featured on the cover of *Using csh and tcsh* is an oystercatcher, a wading shore bird that is found on every continent but Antarctica. This striking-looking bird has sharply contrasting black and white plumage, scarlet irises, and a long, bright orange bill that is compressed along the sides.

Most oystercatchers form permanent pair bonds. Their breeding grounds are usually a short distance inland from their feeding grounds, and many pairs return to the same breeding ground each spring. The incubation period is 25 to 28 days, with an average of three eggs per clutch. Oystercatchers are unusual among shore birds in that they feed their young for the first six weeks or so. The diet of oystercatchers consists mainly of bivalve mollusks, such as cockles, mussels, and oysters, crabs, periwinkles, lugworms, and earthworms. Chicks learn to hunt for worms as young as six weeks, using the Herbst's corpuscles, tactile organs on their bills, to locate them in the sand. However, it can take years for an oystercatcher to perfect the technique of opening mollusk shells.

There are two methods of opening mollusk shells: hammering and stabbing. In hammering, the shell is carried to a rock and repeatedly hammered until opened. In stabbing, the oystercatcher uses its long bill to pry open a shell that is agape and to sever the adductor muscles that clamp the shell shut. Individual oystercatchers are either hammerers or stabbers, depending on the method they were taught when young. Similarly, oystercatchers are either mollusk eaters or crab eaters, again depending on their upbringing. Mollusk-eating chicks have been known to be frightened by crabs.

Edie Freedman designed the cover of this book, using a 19th-century engraving from the Dover Pictorial Archive. The cover layout was produced with Quark XPress 3.3 using the ITC Garamond font.

The inside layout was designed by Edie Freedman and Nancy Priest and implemented in gtroff by Lenny Muellner. The text and heading fonts are ITC Garamond Light and Garamond Book. The illustrations that appear in the book were created in Macromedia Freehand 5.0 by Chris Reilley. The colophon was written by Clairemarie Fisher O'Leary.

More Titles from O'REILLY™

Basics

Learning the UNIX Operating System

By Grace Todino, John Strang & Jerry Peek
3rd Edition August 1993
108 pages, ISBN 1-56592-060-0

If you are new to UNIX, this concise introduction will tell you just what you need to get started and no more. Why wade through a 600-page book when you can begin working productively in a matter of minutes? It's an ideal primer for Mac and PC users of the Internet who need to know a little bit about UNIX on the systems they visit.

This book is the most effective introduction to UNIX in print. The third edition has been updated and expanded to provide increased coverage of window systems and networking. It's a handy book for someone just starting with UNIX, as well as someone who encounters a UNIX system as a "visitor" via remote login over the Internet.

Learning GNU Emacs, 2nd Edition

By Debra Cameron, Bill Rosenblatt & Eric Raymond
2nd Edition Fall 1996
540 pages (est.), ISBN 1-56592-152-6

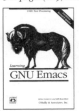

An introduction to Version 19.29 of the GNU Emacs editor, one of the most widely used and powerful editors available under UNIX. Provides a solid introduction to basic editing, a look at several important "editing modes" (special Emacs features for editing specific types of documents, including email, Usenet News, and the World Wide Web), and a brief introduction to customization and Emacs LISP programming. The book is aimed at new Emacs users, whether or not they are programmers. Includes quick-reference card.

Learning the bash Shell

By Cameron Newham & Bill Rosenblatt
1st Edition October 1995
310 pages, ISBN 1-56592-147-X

Whether you want to use *bash* for its programming features or its user interface, you'll find *Learning the bash Shell* a valuable guide. If you're new to shell programming, it provides an excellent introduction, covering everything from the most basic to the most advanced features, like signal handling and command line processing. If you've been writing shell scripts for years, it offers a great way to find out what the new shell offers.

Learning the Korn Shell

By Bill Rosenblatt
1st Edition June 1993
360 pages, ISBN 1-56592-054-6

This Nutshell Handbook® is a thorough introduction to the Korn shell, both as a user interface and as a programming language.

The Korn shell is a program that interprets UNIX commands. It has many features that aren't found in other shells, including command history. This book provides a clear and concise explanation of the Korn shell's features. It explains *ksh* string operations, co-processes, signals and signal handling, and command-line interpretation. The book also includes real-life programming examples and a Korn shell debugger called *kshdb*, the only known implementation of a shell debugger anywhere.

Using csh and tcsh

By Paul DuBois
1st Edition August 1995
242 pages, ISBN 1-56592-132-1

Using csh and tcsh describes from the beginning how to use these shells interactively to get your work done faster with less typing. You'll learn how to make your prompt tell you where you are (no more pwd); use what you've typed before (history); type long command lines with very few keystrokes (command and filename completion); remind yourself of filenames when in the middle of typing a command; and edit a botched command without retyping it.

Learning the vi Editor

By Linda Lamb
5th Edition October 1990
192 pages, ISBN 0-937175-67-6

A complete guide to text editing with *vi*, the editor available on nearly every UNIX system. Early chapters cover the basics; later chapters explain more advanced editing tools, such as *ex* commands and global search and replacement.

For information: **800-998-9938**, 707-829-0515; **info@ora.com; http://www.ora.com/**
To order: **800-889-8969** (credit card orders only); **order@ora.com**

Basics *(continued)*

sed & awk

By Dale Dougherty
1st Edition November 1990
414 pages, ISBN 0-937175-59-5

For people who create and modify text files, *sed* and *awk* are power tools for editing. Most of the things that you can do with these programs can be done interactively with a text editor. However, using *sed* and *awk* can save many hours of repetitive work in achieving the same result.

This book contains a comprehensive treatment of *sed* and *awk* syntax. It emphasizes the kinds of practical problems that *sed* and *awk* can help users to solve, with many useful example scripts and programs.

SCO UNIX in a Nutshell

By Ellie Cutler & the staff of O'Reilly & Associates
1st Edition February 1994
590 pages, ISBN 1-56592-037-6

The desktop reference to SCO UNIX and Open Desktop®, this version of *UNIX in a Nutshell* shows you what's under the hood of your SCO system. It isn't a scaled-down quick reference of common commands, but a complete reference containing all user, programming, administration, and networking commands.

"A very handy desktop reference to have . . . faster than search[ing] through pages of man references. A valuable and handy guide."—Rob Slade, alt.books.reviews

UNIX in a Nutshell: System V Edition

By Daniel Gilly & the staff of O'Reilly & Associates
2nd Edition June 1992
444 pages, ISBN 1-56592-001-5

You may have seen UNIX quick-reference guides, but you've never seen anything like *UNIX in a Nutshell*. Not a scaled-down quick reference of common commands, *UNIX in a Nutshell* is a complete reference containing all commands and options, along with generous descriptions and examples that put the commands in context. For all but the thorniest UNIX problems, this one reference should be all the documentation you need. Covers System V, Releases 3 and 4, and Solaris 2.0.

What You Need to Know: When You Can't Find Your UNIX System Administrator

By Linda Mui
1st Edition April 1995
156 pages, ISBN 1-56592-104-6

This book is written for UNIX users, who are often cast adrift in a confusing environment. It provides the background and practical solutions you need to solve problems you're likely to encounter — problems with logging in, printing, sharing files, running programs, managing space resources, etc. It also describes the kind of info to gather when you're asking for a diagnosis from a busy sys admin. And, it gives you a list of site-specific information that you should know, as well as a place to write it down.

Volume 3M: X Window System User's Guide,

Motif Edition
By Valerie Quercia & Tim O'Reilly
2nd Edition January 1993
956 pages, ISBN 1-56592-015-5

The *X Window System User's Guide, Motif Edition,* orients the new user to window system concepts and provides detailed tutorials for many client programs, including the *xterm* terminal emulator and the window manager. Building on this basic knowledge, later chapters explain how to customize the X environment and provide sample configurations.

This alternative edition of the *User's Guide* highlights the Motif window manager, for users of the Motif graphical user interface. Revised for Motif 1.2 and X11 Release 5.

Material covered in this second edition includes:
- Overview of the X Color Management System (Xcms)
- Creating your own Xcms color database
- Tutorials for two "color editors": *xcolor edit* and *xtici*
- Using the X font server
- Tutorial for *editres*, a resource editor
- Extensive coverage of the new implementations of *bitmap* and *xmag*
- Overview of internationalization features
- Features common to Motif 1.2 applications: tear-off menus and drag-and-drop

Perl

Programming Perl

By Larry Wall, Randal L. Schwartz & Tom Christiansen
2nd Edition September 1996
676 pages, ISBN 1-56592-149-6

This heavily revised second edition of *Programming Perl* contains a full explanation of Perl version 5.002 features. It's the authoritative guide to Perl—the scripting utility now established as the World Wide Web programming tool of choice. The book is coauthored by Larry Wall, the creator of Perl.

"The Perl book is splendid. It is clearly written and very craftily draws the reader into wanting to learn more."—John Ward, Professor, Oxford College

Learning Perl

By Randal L. Schwartz, Foreword by Larry Wall
1st Edition November 1993
274 pages, ISBN 1-56592-042-2

Learning Perl is ideal for system administrators, programmers, and anyone else wanting a down-to-earth introduction to this useful language. Written by a Perl trainer, its aim is to make a competent, hands-on Perl programmer out of the reader as quickly as possible. The book takes a tutorial approach and includes hundreds of short code examples, along with some lengthy ones. The relatively inexperienced programmer will find *Learning Perl* easily accessible.

Each chapter of the book includes practical programming exercises. Solutions are presented for all exercises.

For a comprehensive and detailed guide to advanced programming with Perl, read O'Reilly's companion book, *Programming Perl*.

"Intended as 'a gentle introduction to Perl'—the Practical Extraction and Report Language of the Unix world, a powerful set of tools to manipulate text. If you're going to spend much time on a Unix operating system, chances are you will want to learn how to use Perl."—Book Review, *ISOC News*

CGI Programming on the World Wide Web

By Shishir Gundavaram
1st Edition March 1996
450 pages, ISBN 1-56592-168-2

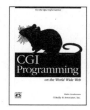

The World Wide Web is more than a place to put up clever documents and pretty pictures. With a little study and practice, you can offer interactive queries and serve instant information from databases, worked up into colorful graphics. That is what the Common Gateway Interface (CGI) offers.

This book offers a comprehensive explanation of CGI and related techniques for people who hold on to the dream of providing their own information servers on the Web. Gundavaram starts at the beginning, explaining the value of CGI and how it works, then moves swiftly into the subtle details of programming. For most of the examples, the book uses the most common platform (UNIX) and the most popular language (Perl) used for CGI programming today. However, it also introduces the essentials of making CGI work with other platforms and languages.

Perl 5 Desktop Reference

By Johan Vromans
1st Edition February 1996
39 pages, ISBN 1-56592-187-9

This booklet gives you quick, well-organized access to the vast array of features in Perl, version 5. Perl is a language for easily manipulating text, files, and processes.

Having first established itself as the UNIX programming tool of choice, Perl is now becoming the World Wide Web programming tool of choice. This guide provides a complete overview of the language, from variables to input and output, from flow control to regular expressions, from functions to document formats—all packed into a convenient, carry-around booklet.

Perl 5 Desktop Reference is the perfect companion to *Learning Perl*, a carefully paced tutorial course by Randal L. Schwartz, and *Programming Perl*, the complete, authoritative reference work coauthored by Perl developer Larry Wall, Tom Christiansen, and Randal L. Schwartz.

For information: **800-998-9938**, 707-829-0515; **info@ora.com; http://www.ora.com/**
To order: **800-889-8969** (credit card orders only); **order@ora.com**

Stay in touch with O'REILLY™

Visit Our Award-Winning World Wide Web Site

http://www.ora.com/

VOTED

> "Top 100 Sites on the Web" —*PC Magazine*
> "Top 5% Websites" —*Point Communications*
> "3-Star site" —*The McKinley Group*

Our Web site contains a library of comprehensive product information (including book excerpts and tables of contents), downloadable software, background articles, interviews with technology leaders, links to relevant sites, book cover art, and more. File us in your Bookmarks or Hotlist!

Join Our Two Email Mailing Lists

LIST #1   **NEW PRODUCT RELEASES:** To receive automatic email with brief descriptions of all new O'Reilly products as they are released, send email to: listproc@online.ora.com and put the following information in the first line of your message (NOT in the Subject: field, which is ignored): **subscribe ora-news "Your Name" of "Your Organization"** (for example: **subscribe ora-news Kris Webber of Fine Enterprises)**

List #2   **O'REILLY EVENTS:** If you'd also like us to send information about trade show events, special promotions, and other O'Reilly events, send email to: **listproc@online.ora.com** and put the following information in the first line of your message (NOT in the Subject: field, which is ignored): **subscribe ora-events "Your Name" of "Your Organization"**

Visit Our Gopher Site

- Connect your Gopher to **gopher.ora.com**, or
- Point your Web browser to **gopher://gopher.ora.com/**, or
- telnet to **gopher.ora.com** (login: **gopher**)

Get Example Files from Our Books Via FTP

There are two ways to access an archive of example files from our books:

REGULAR FTP — ftp to: **ftp.ora.com** (login: **anonymous**—use your email address as the password) or point your Web browser to: **ftp://ftp.ora.com/**

FTPMAIL — Send an email message to: **ftpmail@online.ora.com** (write "help" in the message body)

Contact Us Via Email

order@ora.com — To place a book or software order online. Good for North American and international customers.

subscriptions@ora.com — To place an order for any of our newsletters or periodicals.

software@ora.com — For general questions and product information about our software.
- Check out O'Reilly Software Online at **http://software.ora.com/** for software and technical support information.
- Registered O'Reilly software users send your questions to **website-support@ora.com**

books@ora.com — General questions about any of our books.

cs@ora.com — For answers to problems regarding your order or our products.

booktech@ora.com — For book content technical questions or corrections.

proposals@ora.com — To submit new book or software proposals to our editors and product managers.

international@ora.com — For information about our international distributors or translation queries.
- For a list of our distributors outside of North America check out: **http://www.ora.com/www/order/country.html**

O'REILLY™

101 Morris Street, Sebastopol, CA 95472 USA
TEL 707-829-0515 or 800-998-9938 (6 A.M. to 5 P.M. PST)
FAX 707-829-0104

TO ORDER: **800-889-8969** (CREDIT CARD ORDERS ONLY); **order@ora.com**; **http://www.ora.com/**
OUR PRODUCTS ARE AVAILABLE AT A BOOKSTORE OR SOFTWARE STORE NEAR YOU.

Titles from O'REILLY™

INTERNET PROGRAMMING

CGI Programming on the
    World Wide Web
Designing for the Web
Exploring Java
HTML: The Definitive Guide
Web Client Programming with Perl
Learning Perl
Programming Perl, 2nd. Edition
    (Fall '96)
JavaScript: The Definitive Guide,
    Beta Edition
WebMaster in a Nutshell
The World Wide Web Journal

USING THE INTERNET

Smileys
The Whole Internet User's Guide
    and Catalog
The Whole Internet for Windows 95
What You Need to Know:
    Using Email Effectively
Marketing on the Internet (Fall '96)
What You Need to Know: Bandits on the
    Information Superhighway

JAVA SERIES

Exploring Java
Java in a Nutshell
Java Language Reference
    (Fall '96 est.)
Java Virtual Machine

WINDOWS

Inside the Windows 95 Registry

SOFTWARE

WebSite™ 1.1
WebSite Professional™
WebBoard™
PolyForm™
Statisphere™

SONGLINE GUIDES

NetLearning
NetSuccess for Realtors
NetActivism
Gif Animation (Fall '96)
Shockwave Studio (Winter '97 est.)

SYSTEM ADMINISTRATION

Building Internet Firewalls
Computer Crime:
    A Crimefighter's Handbook
Computer Security Basics
DNS and BIND
Essential System Administration,
    2nd Edition
Getting Connected:
    The Internet at 56K and Up
Linux Network Administrator's Guide
Managing Internet Information Services
Managing Usenet (Fall '96)
Managing NFS and NIS
Networking Personal Computers
    with TCP/IP
Practical UNIX & Internet Security
PGP: Pretty Good Privacy
sendmail
System Performance Tuning
TCP/IP Network Administration
termcap & terminfo
Using & Managing UUCP
Volume 8: X Window System
    Administrator's Guide

UNIX

Exploring Expect
Learning GNU Emacs, 2nd Edition
    (Fall '96)
Learning the bash Shell
Learning the Korn Shell
Learning the UNIX Operating System
Learning the vi Editor
Linux in a Nutshell (Fall '96 est.)
Making TeX Work
Linux Multimedia Guide (Fall '96)
Running Linux, 2nd Edition
Running Linux Companion
    CD-ROM, 2nd Edition
SCO UNIX in a Nutshell
sed & awk
UNIX in a Nutshell: System V Edition
UNIX Power Tools
UNIX Systems Programming
Using csh and tsch
What You Need to Know:
    When You Can't Find Your
    UNIX System Administrator

PROGRAMMING

Applying RCS and SCCS
C++: The Core Language
Checking C Programs with lint
DCE Security Programming
Distributing Applications Across
    DCE and Windows NT
Encyclopedia of Graphics File
    Formats, 2nd Edition
Guide to Writing DCE Applications
lex & yacc
Managing Projects with make
ORACLE Performance Tuning
ORACLE PL/SQL Programming
Porting UNIX Software
POSIX Programmer's Guide
POSIX.4: Programming for
    the Real World
Power Programming with RPC
Practical C Programming
Practical C++ Programming
Programming Python (Fall '96)
Programming with curses
Programming with GNU Software
    (Fall '96 est.)
Pthreads Programming
Software Portability with imake
Understanding DCE
Understanding Japanese Information
    Processing
UNIX Systems Programming for SVR4

BERKELEY 4.4 SOFTWARE DISTRIBUTION

4.4BSD System Manager's Manual
4.4BSD User's Reference Manual
4.4BSD User's Supplementary
    Documents
4.4BSD Programmer's Reference
    Manual
4.4BSD Programmer's Supplementary
    Documents

X PROGRAMMING
THE X WINDOW SYSTEM

Volume 0: X Protocol Reference Manual
Volume 1: Xlib Programming Manual
Volume 2: Xlib Reference Manual
Volume. 3M: X Window System
    User's Guide, Motif Edition
Volume. 4: X Toolkit Intrinsics
    Programming Manual
Volume 4M: X Toolkit Intrinsics
    Programming Manual,
    Motif Edition
Volume 5: X Toolkit Intrinsics
    Reference Manual
Volume 6A: Motif Programming
    Manual
Volume 6B: Motif Reference Manual
Volume 6C: Motif Tools
Volume 8 : X Window System
    Administrator's Guide
Programmer's Supplement for Release 6
X User Tools (with CD-ROM)
The X Window System in a Nutshell

HEALTH, CAREER, & BUSINESS

Building a Successful Software Business
The Computer User's Survival Guide
Dictionary of Computer Terms
The Future Does Not Compute
Love Your Job!
Publishing with CD-ROM

TRAVEL

Travelers' Tales: Brazil (Fall '96)
Travelers' Tales: Food (Fall '96)
Travelers' Tales: France
Travelers' Tales: Hong Kong
Travelers' Tales: India
Travelers' Tales: Mexico
Travelers' Tales: San Francisco
Travelers' Tales: Spain
Travelers' Tales: Thailand
Travelers' Tales: A Woman's World

International Distributors

Customers outside North America can now order O'Reilly & Associates books through the following distributors. They offer our international customers faster order processing, more bookstores, increased representation at tradeshows worldwide, and the high-quality, responsive service our customers have come to expect.

EUROPE, MIDDLE EAST AND NORTHERN AFRICA *(except Germany, Switzerland, and Austria)*

INQUIRIES
International Thomson Publishing Europe
Berkshire House
168-173 High Holborn
London WC1V 7AA, United Kingdom
Telephone: 44-171-497-1422
Fax: 44-171-497-1426
Email: **itpint@itps.co.uk**

ORDERS
International Thomson Publishing Services, Ltd.
Cheriton House, North Way
Andover, Hampshire SP10 5BE,
United Kingdom
Telephone: 44-264-342-832 (UK orders)
Telephone: 44-264-342-806 (outside UK)
Fax: 44-264-364418 (UK orders)
Fax: 44-264-342761 (outside UK)
UK & Eire orders: **itpuk@itps.co.uk**
International orders: **itpint@itps.co.uk**

GERMANY, SWITZERLAND, AND AUSTRIA

International Thomson Publishing GmbH
O'Reilly International Thomson Verlag
Königswinterer Straße 418
53227 Bonn, Germany
Telephone: 49-228-97024 0
Fax: 49-228-441342
Email: **anfragen@arade.ora.de**

AUSTRALIA

WoodsLane Pty. Ltd.
7/5 Vuko Place, Warriewood NSW 2102
P.O. Box 935, Mona Vale NSW 2103
Australia
Telephone: 61-2-9970-5111
Fax: 61-2-9970-5002
Email: **info@woodslane.com.au**

NEW ZEALAND

WoodsLane New Zealand Ltd.
21 Cooks Street (P.O. Box 575)
Wanganui, New Zealand
Telephone: 64-6-347-6543
Fax: 64-6-345-4840
Email: **info@woodslane.com.au**

ASIA *(except Japan & India)*

INQUIRIES
International Thomson Publishing Asia
60 Albert Street #15-01
Albert Complex
Singapore 189969
Telephone: 65-336-6411
Fax: 65-336-7411

ORDERS
Telephone: 65-336-6411
Fax: 65-334-1617

JAPAN

O'Reilly Japan, Inc.
Kiyoshige Building 2F
12-Banchi, Sanei-cho
Shinjuku-ku
Tokyo 160 Japan
Telephone: 81-3-3356-5227
Fax: 81-3-3356-5261
Email: **kenji@ora.com**

INDIA

Computer Bookshop (India) PVT. LTD.
190 Dr. D.N. Road, Fort
Bombay 400 001
India
Telephone: 91-22-207-0989
Fax: 91-22-262-3551
Email: **cbsbom@giasbm01.vsnl.net.in**

THE AMERICAS

O'Reilly & Associates, Inc.
101 Morris Street
Sebastopol, CA 95472 U.S.A.
Telephone: 707-829-0515
Telephone: 800-998-9938 (U.S. & Canada)
Fax: 707-829-0104
Email: **order@ora.com**

SOUTHERN AFRICA

International Thomson Publishing Southern Africa
Building 18, Constantia Park
240 Old Pretoria Road
P.O. Box 2459
Halfway House, 1685 South Africa
Telephone: 27-11-805-4819
Fax: 27-11-805-3648

O'REILLY™

TO ORDER: **800-889-8969** (CREDIT CARD ORDERS ONLY); **order@ora.com**; **http://www.ora.com**
OUR PRODUCTS ARE AVAILABLE AT A BOOKSTORE OR SOFTWARE STORE NEAR YOU.